TOH

THE TRY ON HAUL MAGAZINE

I0440312

Try On Haul :

"A young and pretty girl that shows in social media clothing she buys, she gets as a gift or she tries as a model, as an influencer or as a new rising star"

Is with love for the art of photography that I make this magazine and photobook to show you my photo sessions with models and influencers from all over the world... **Try on Haul** *Style*

I hope you enjoy the images and much as I enjoyed doing them.

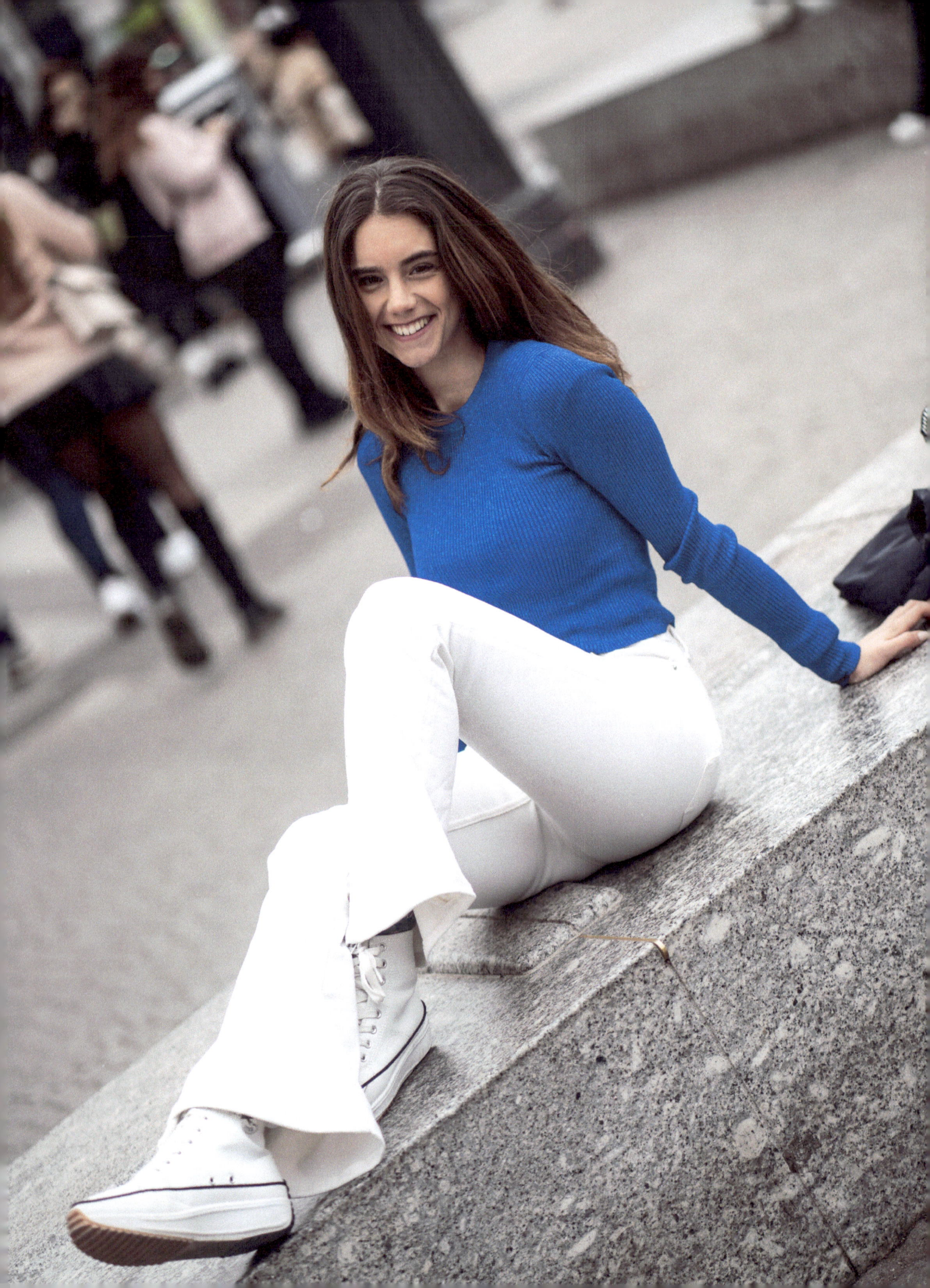

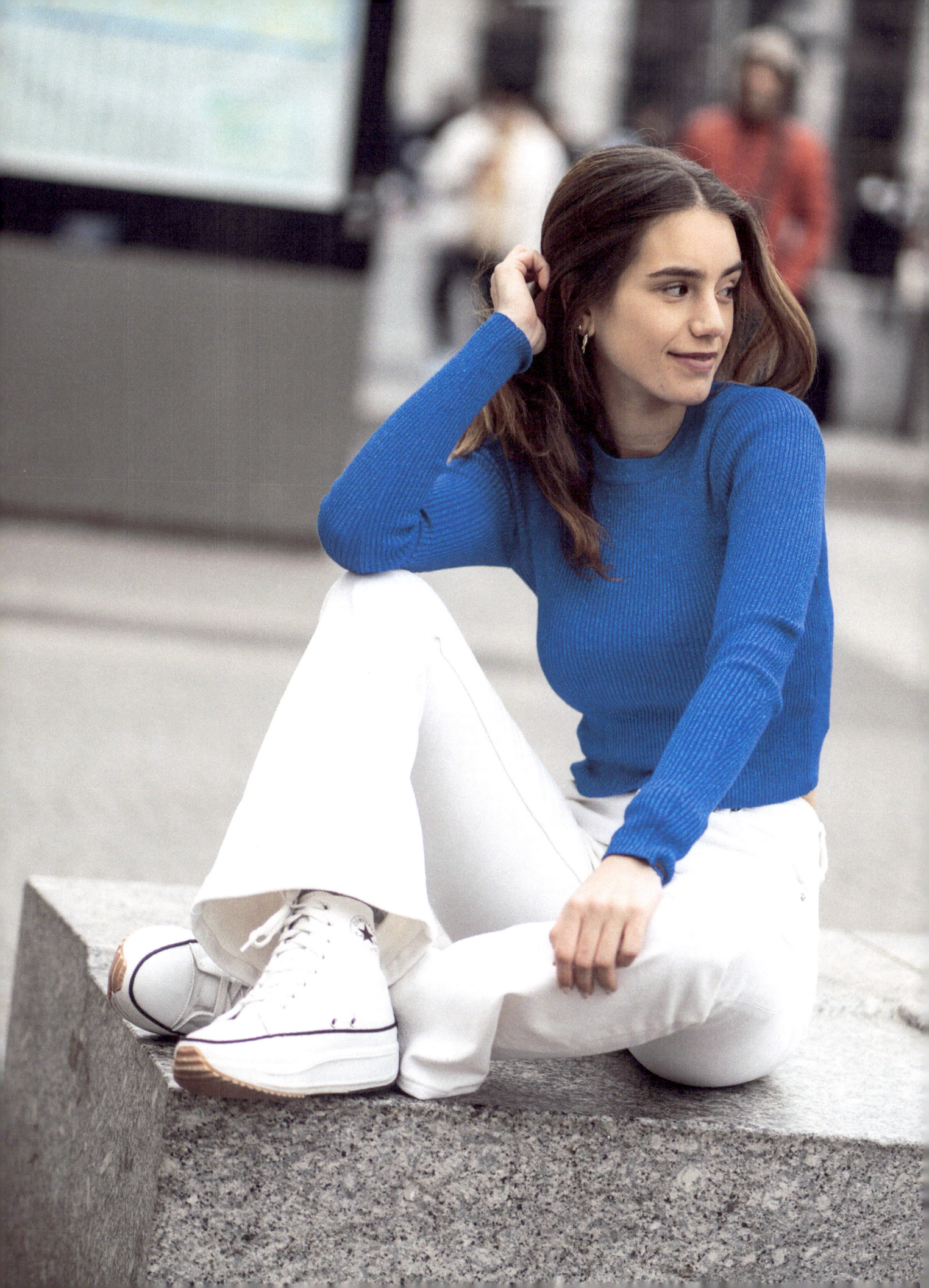

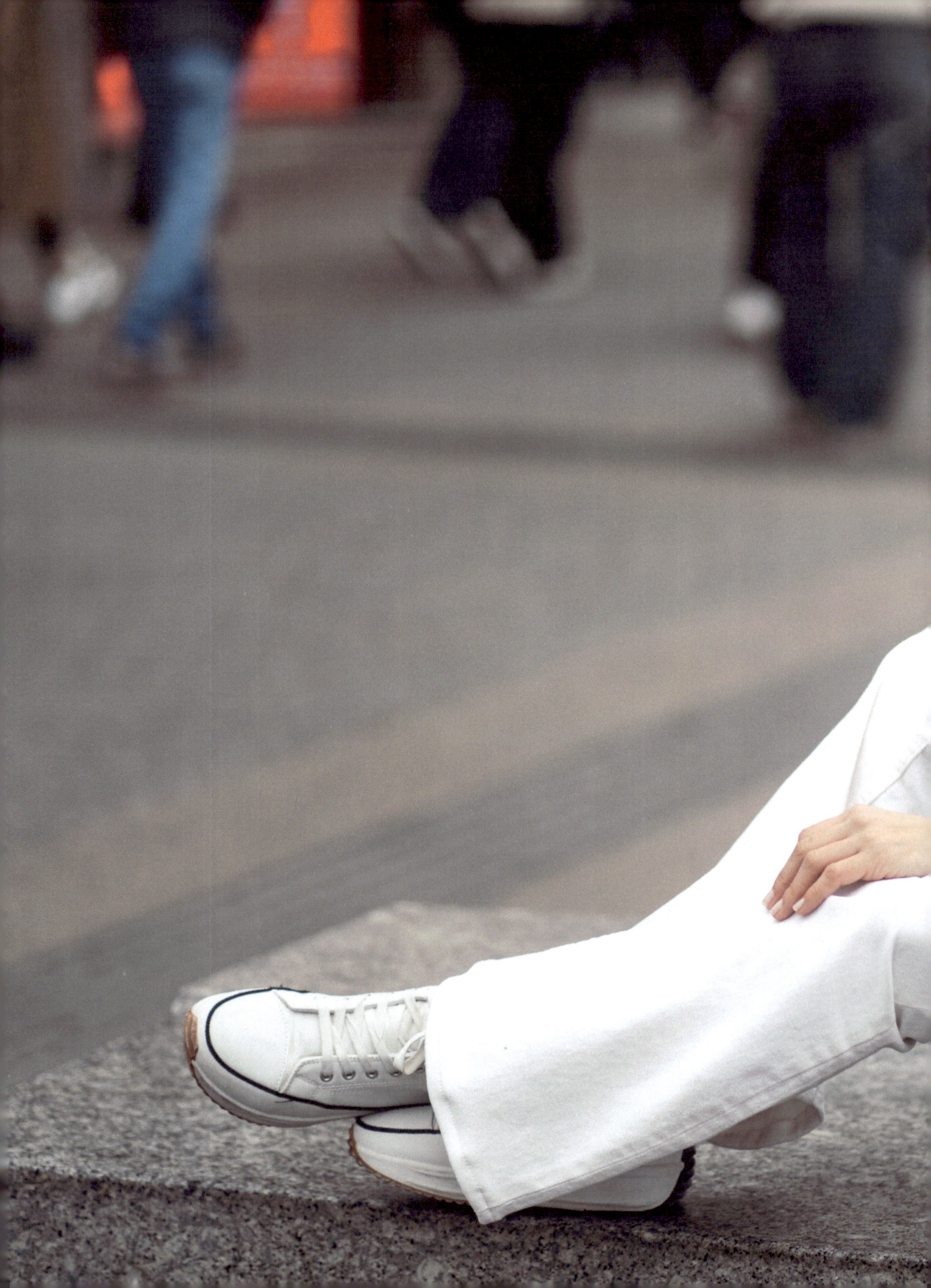

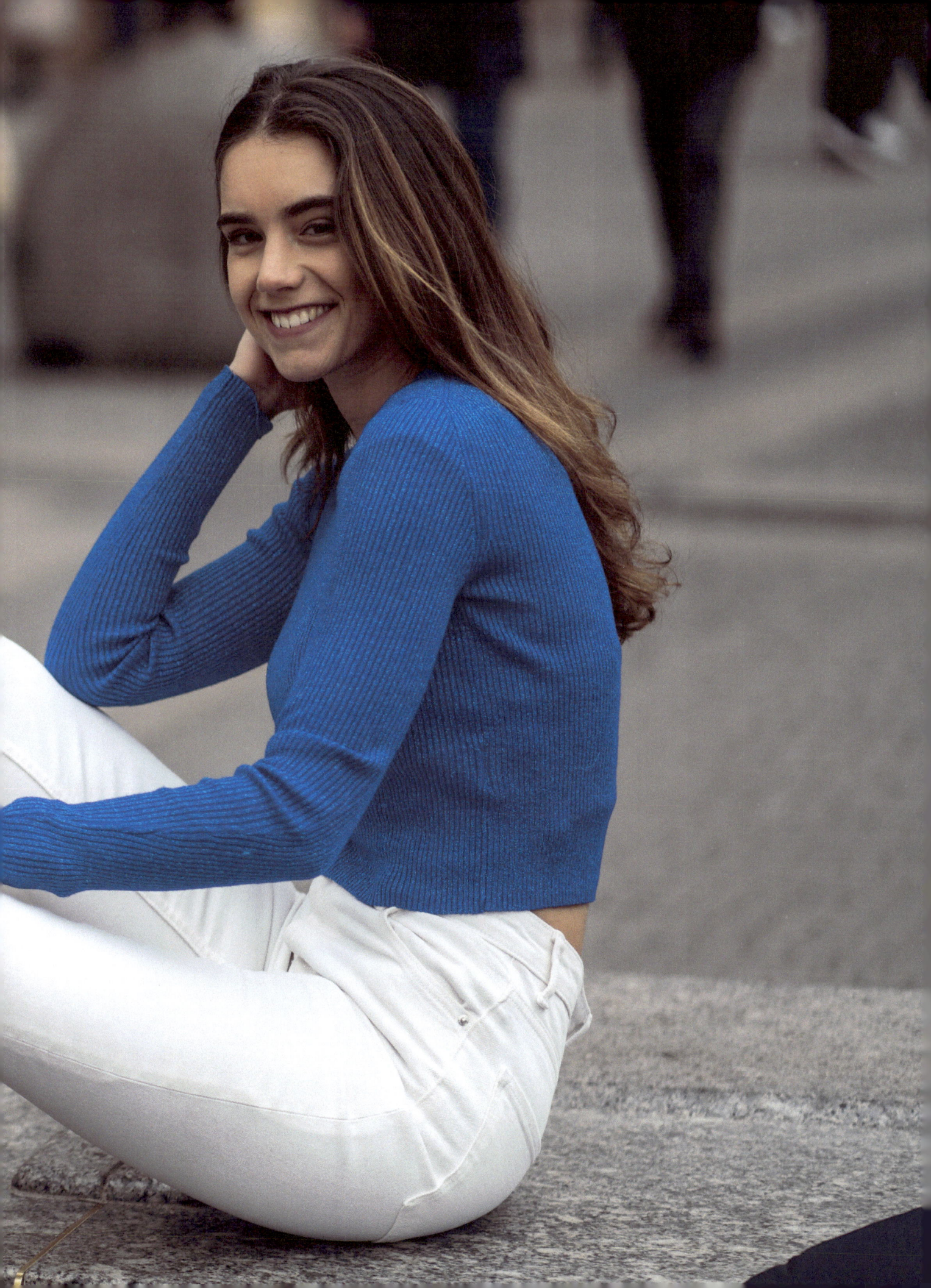

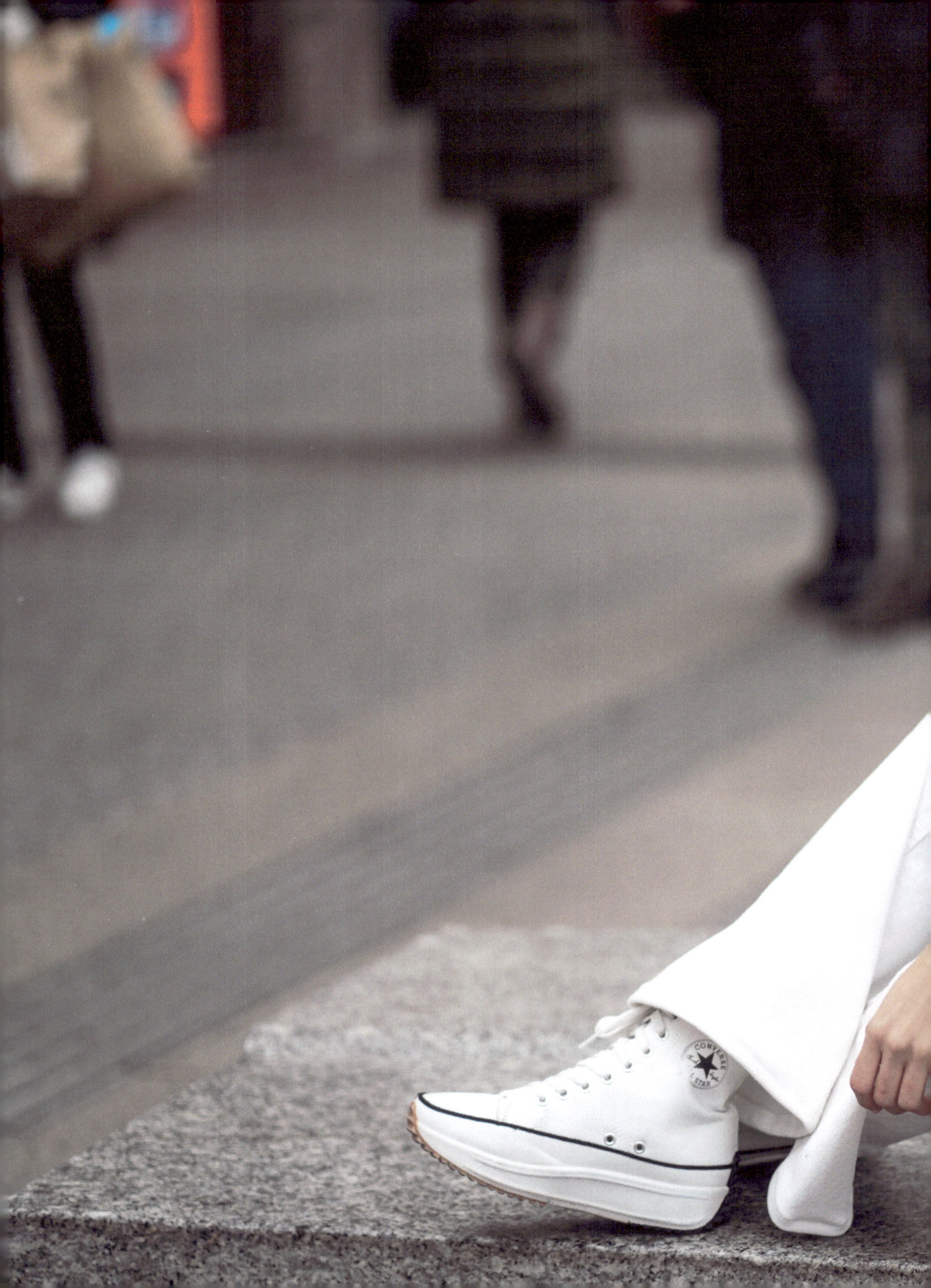

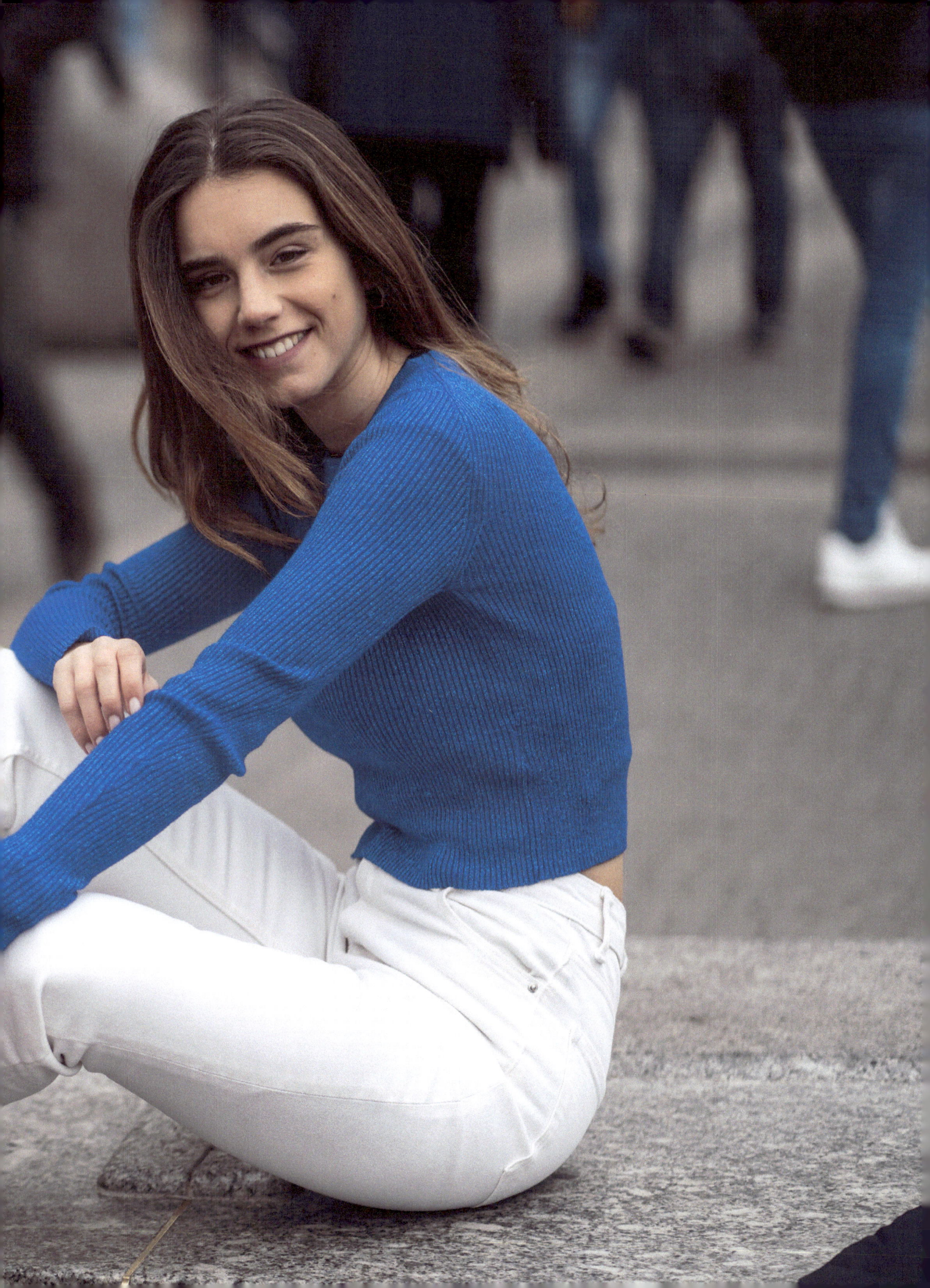

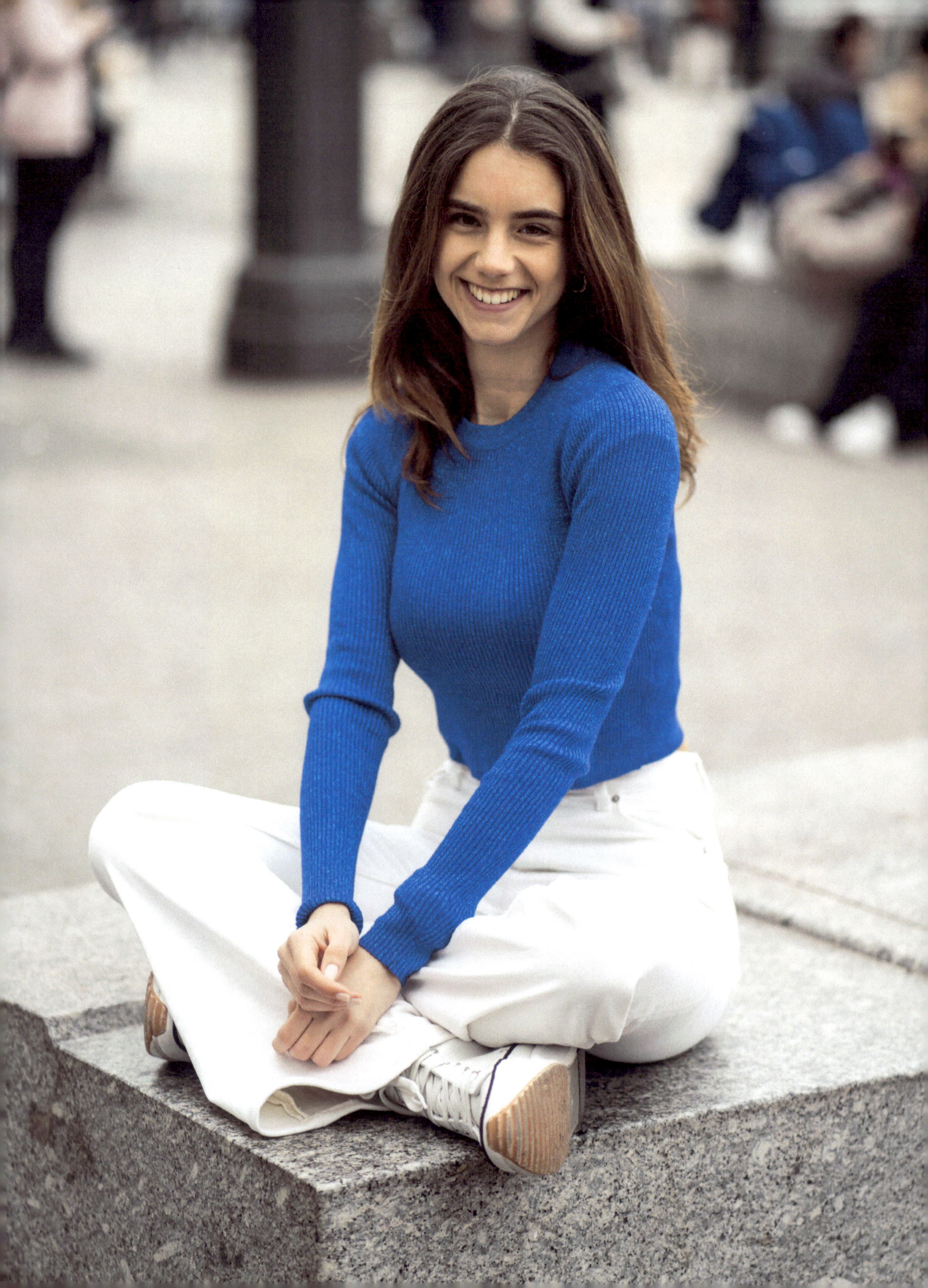

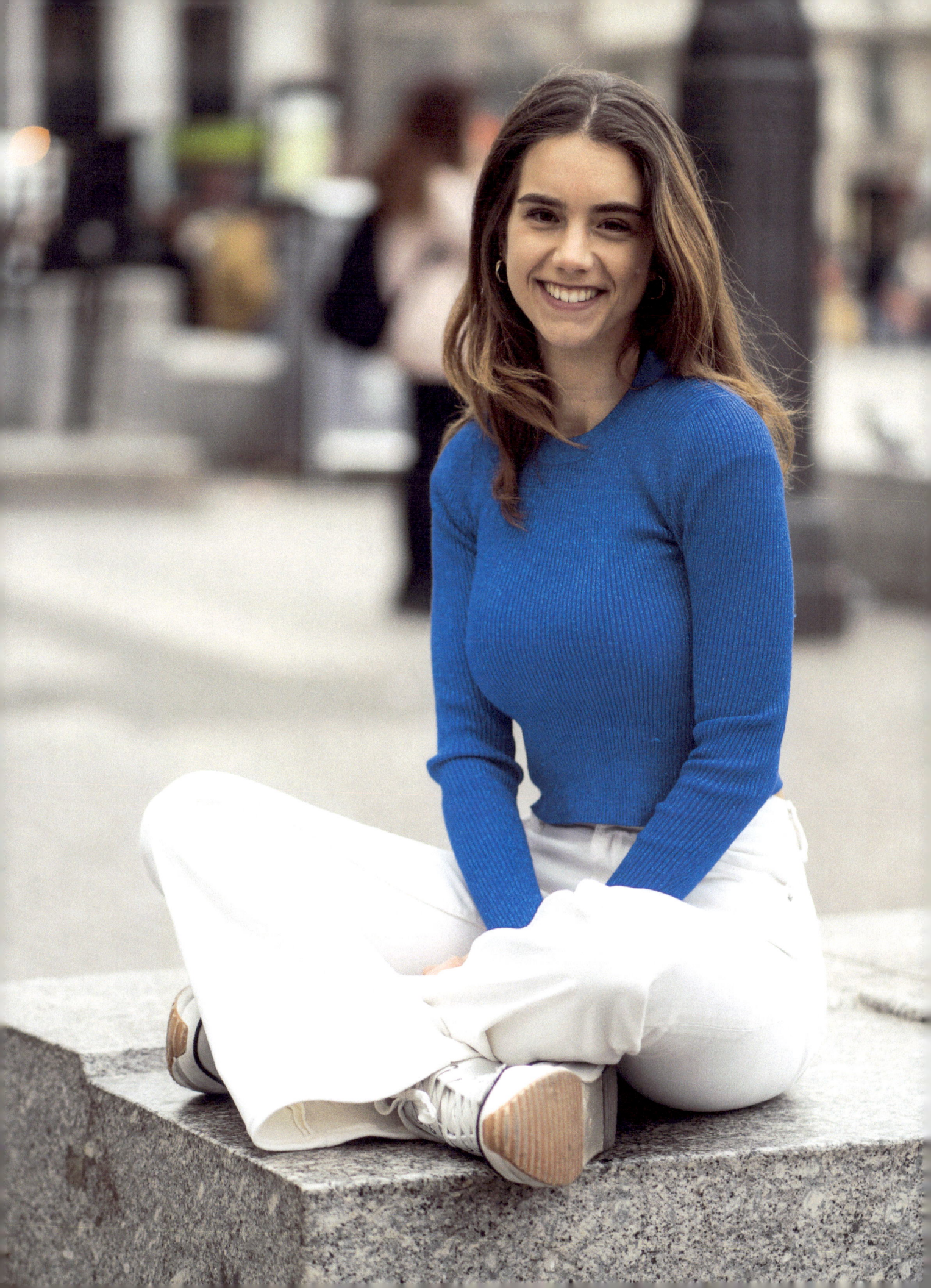

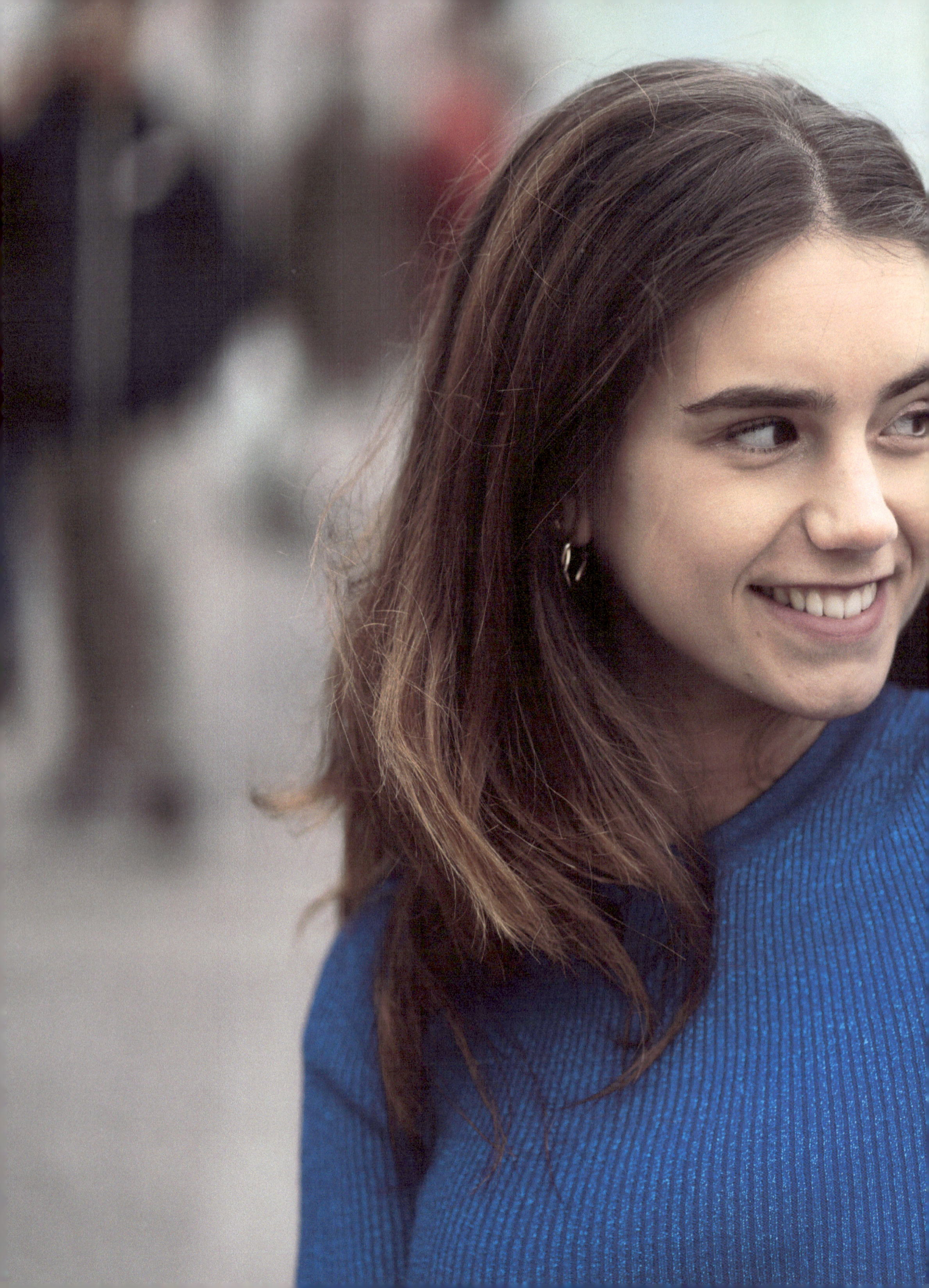

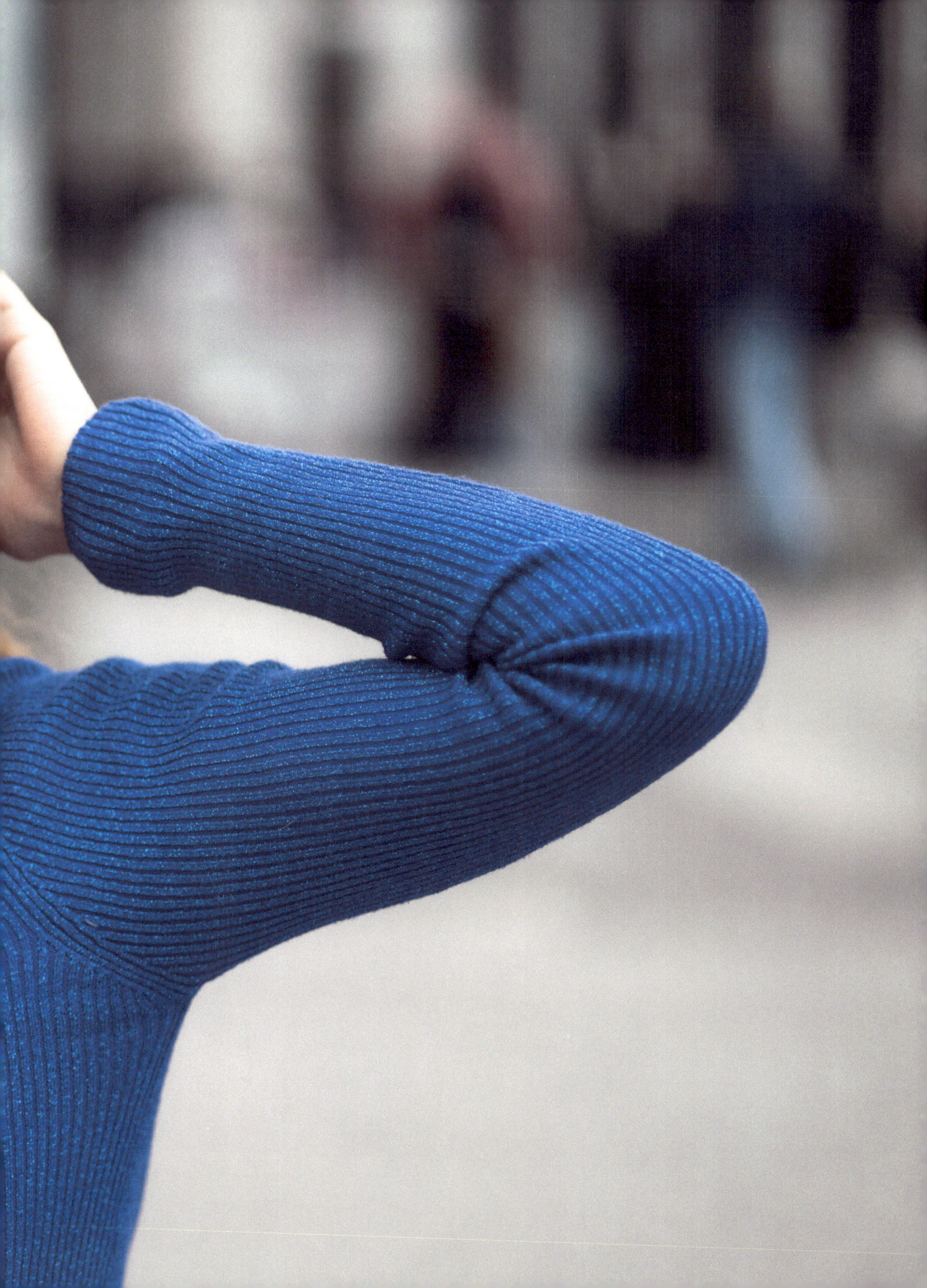

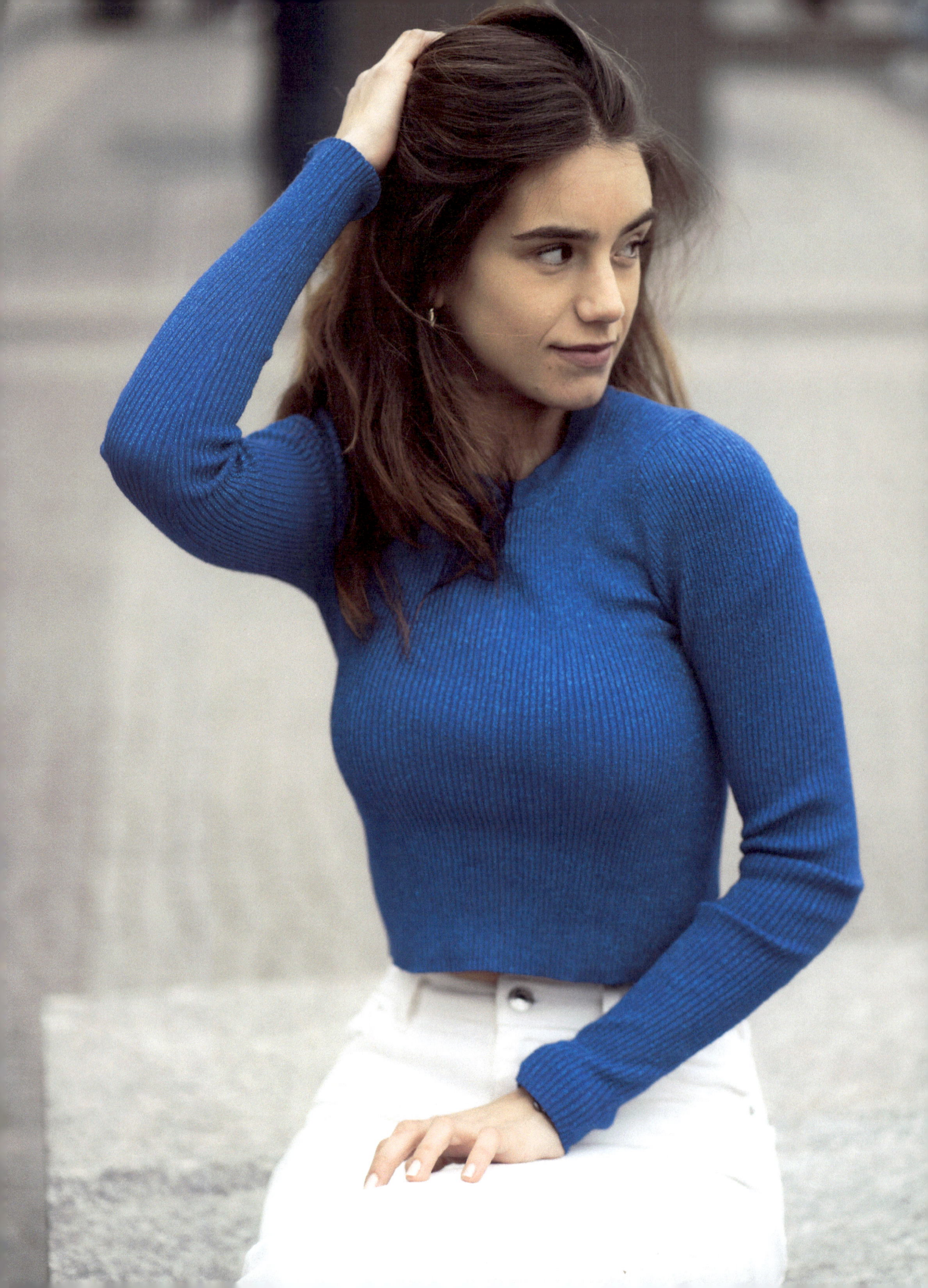

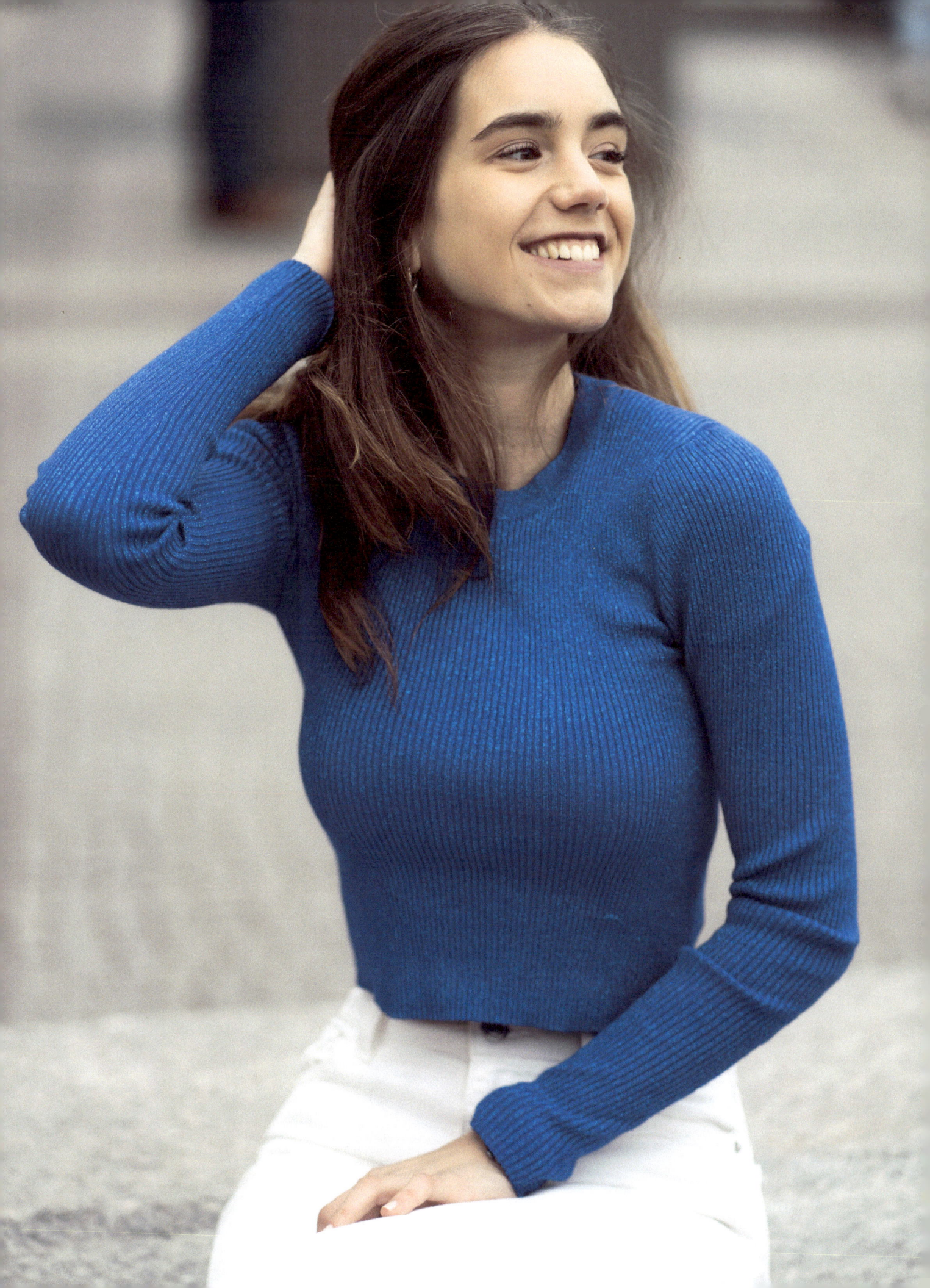

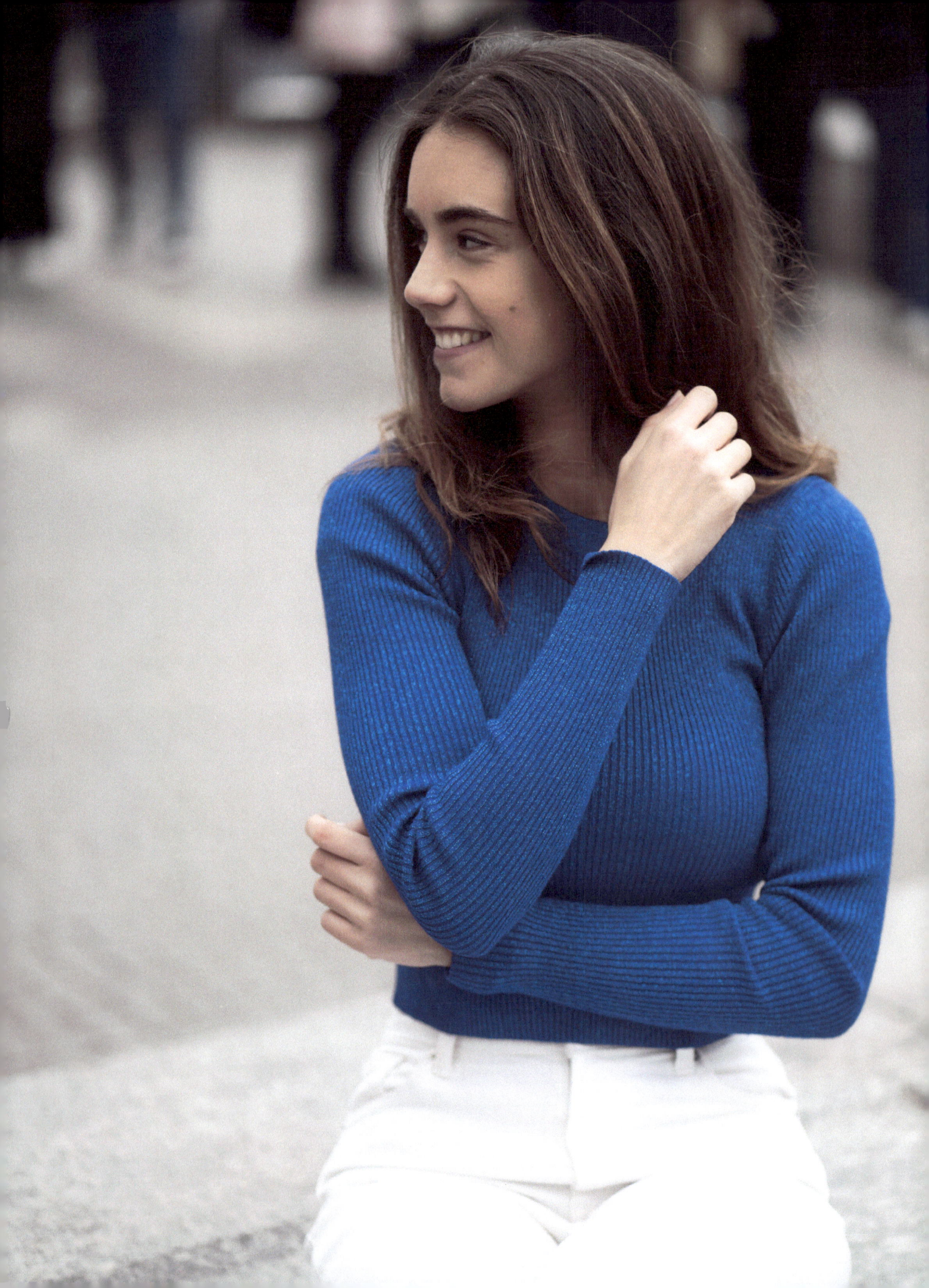

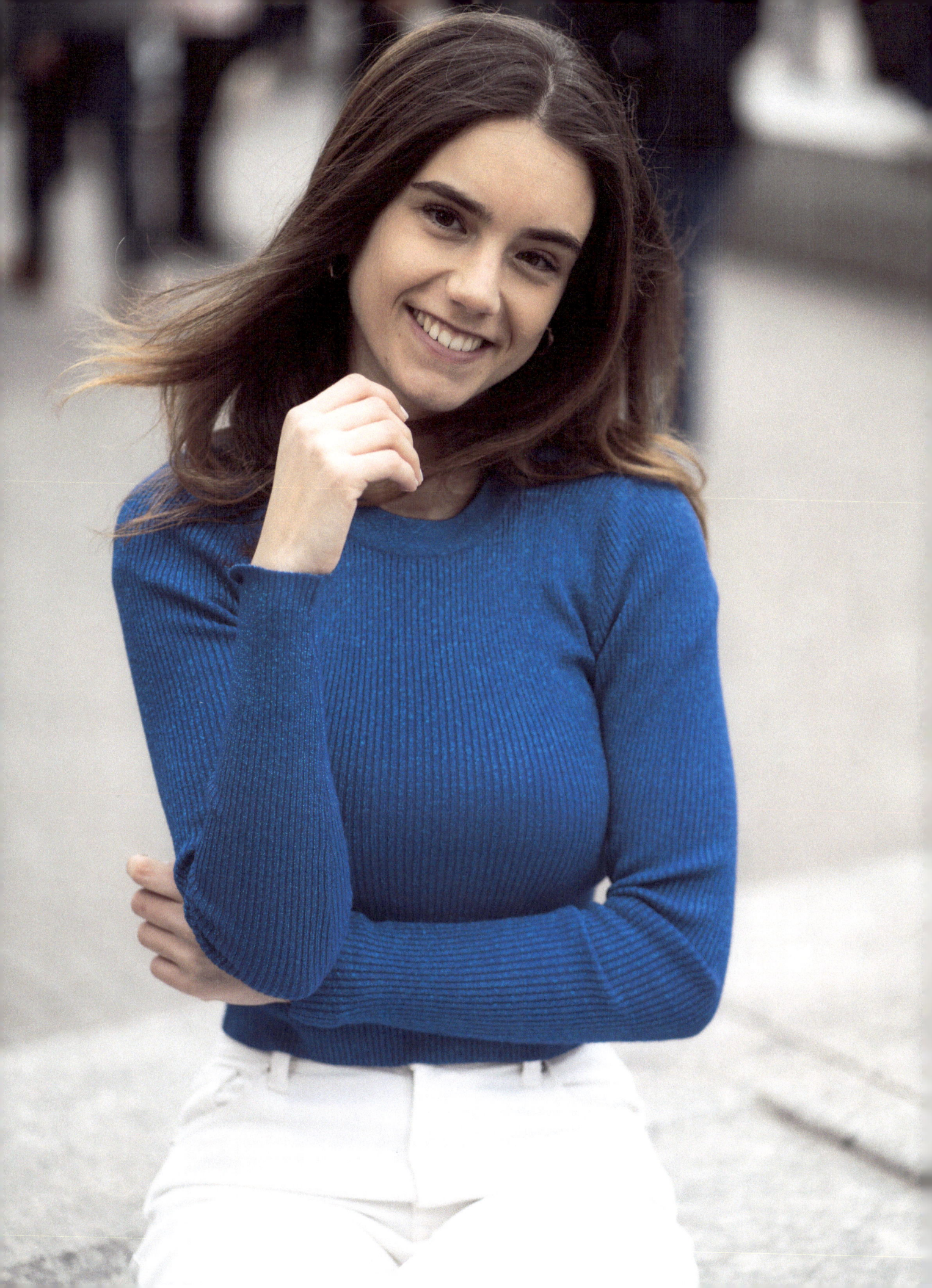

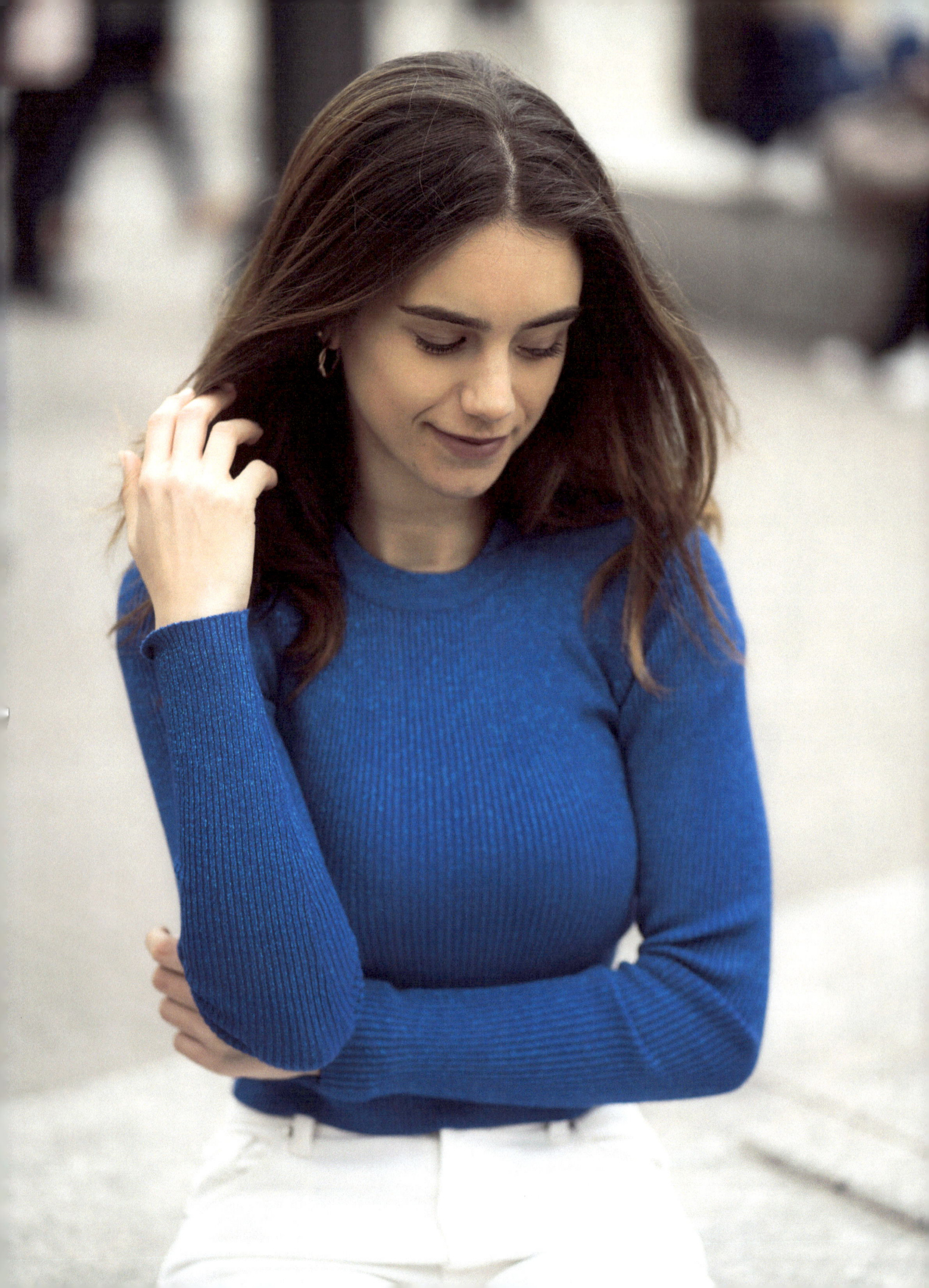

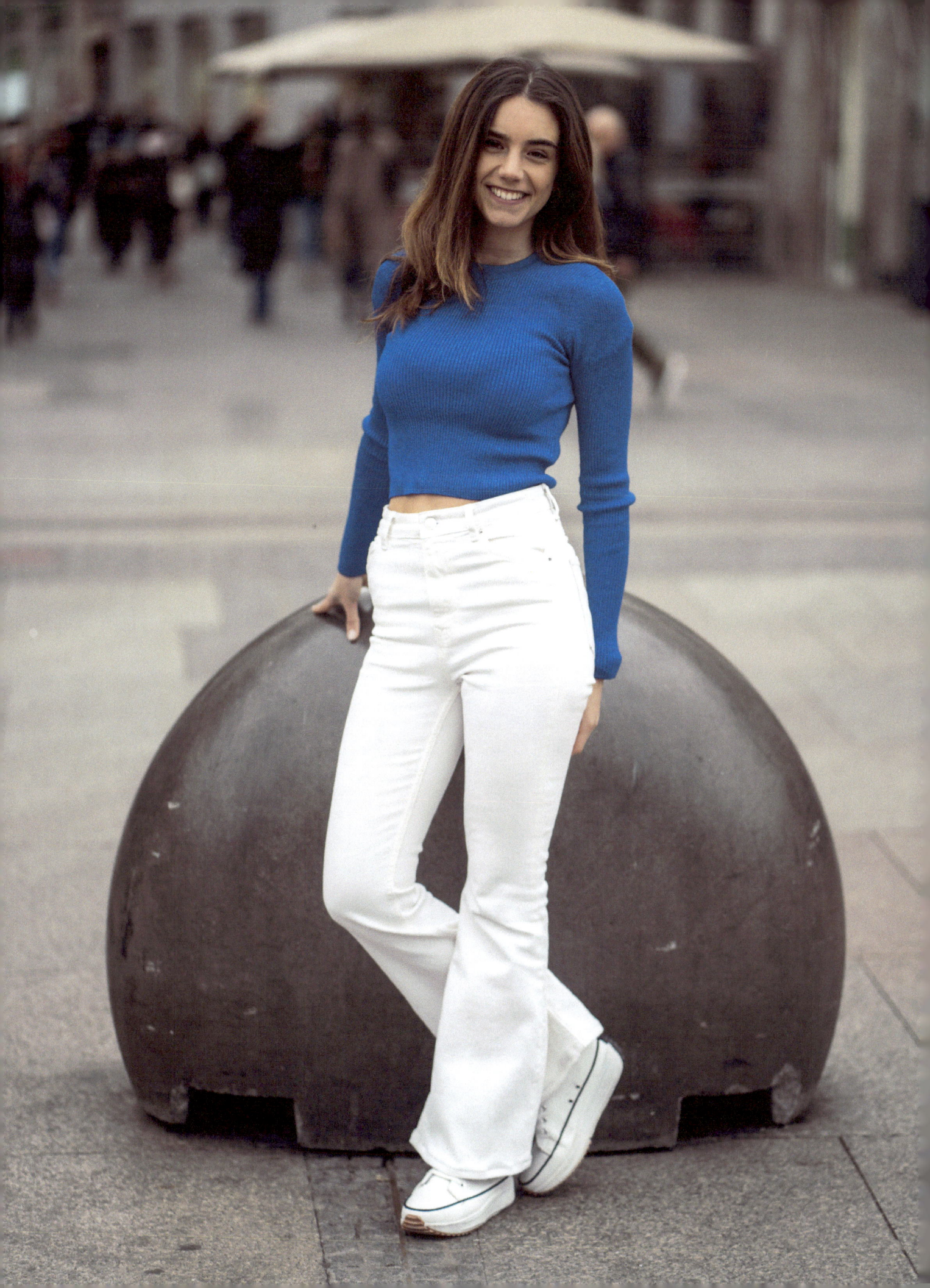

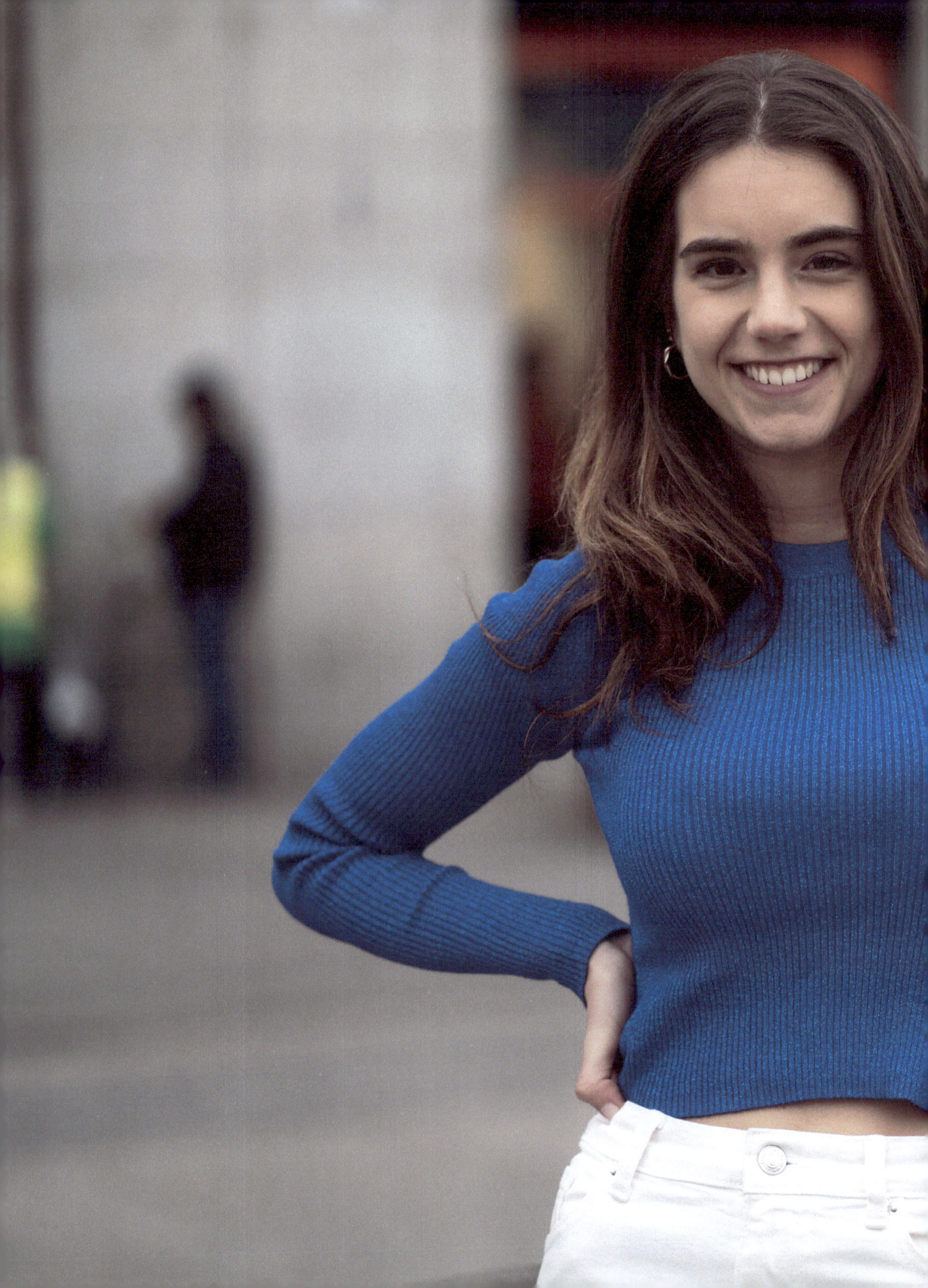

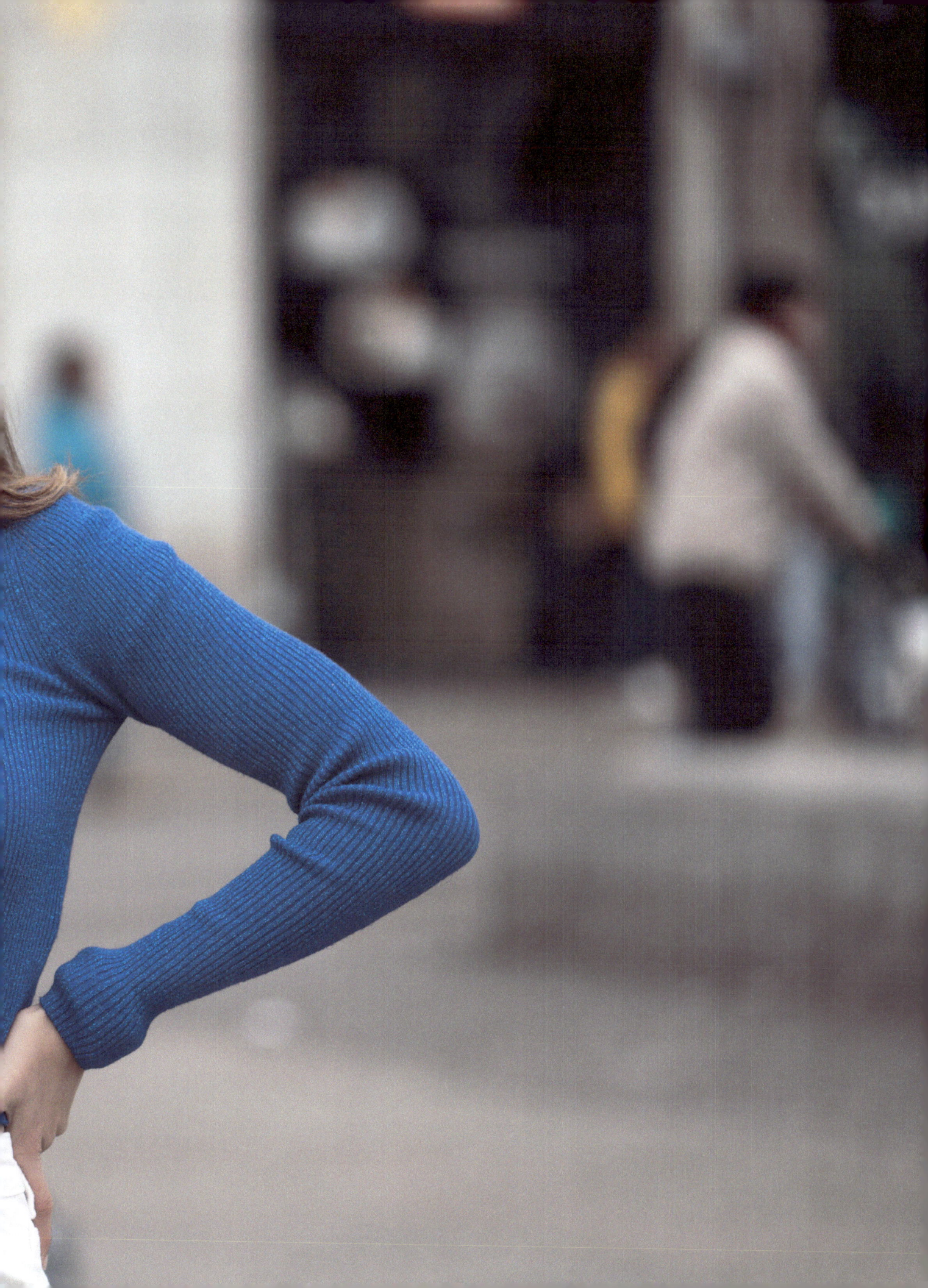

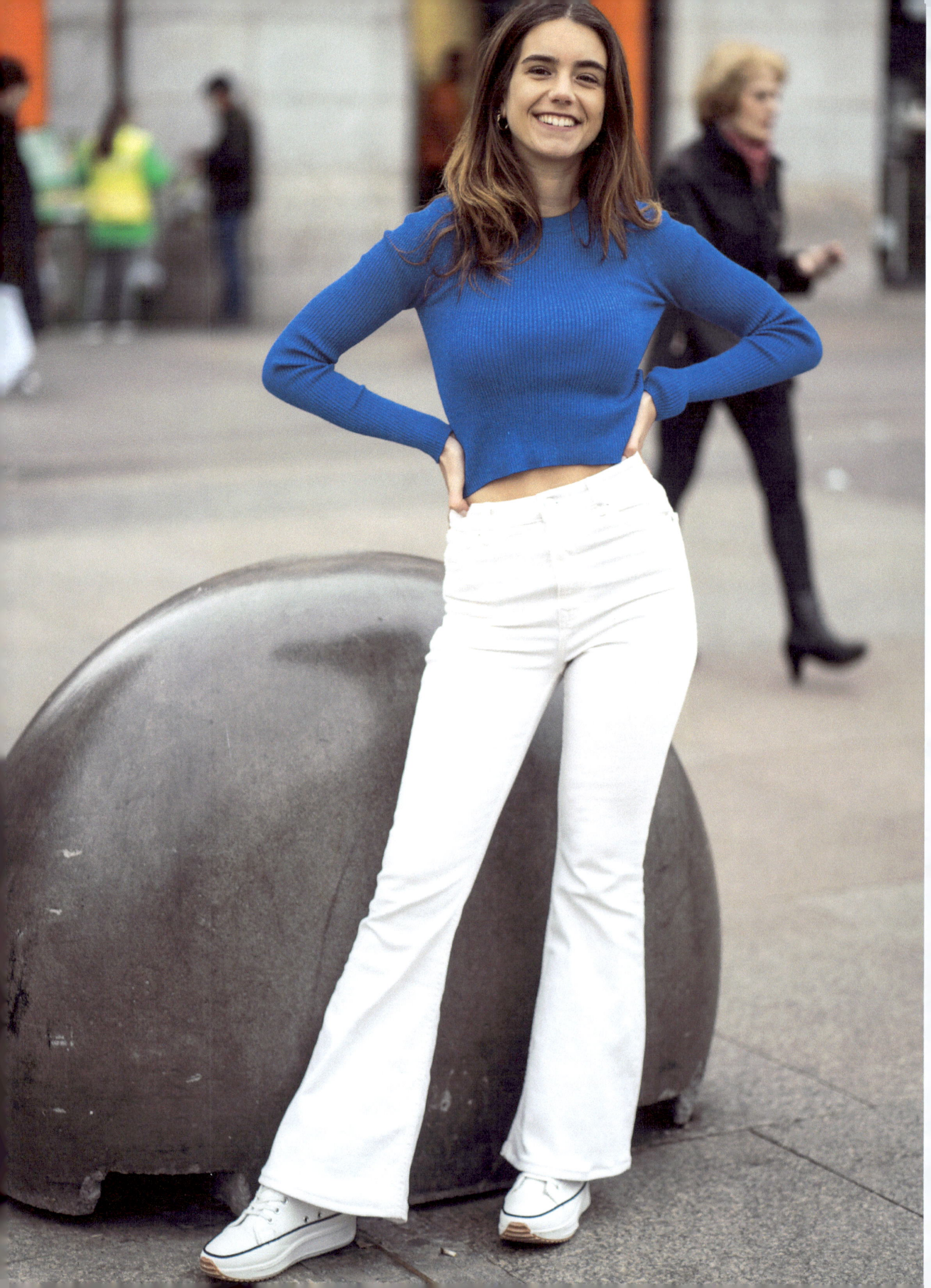

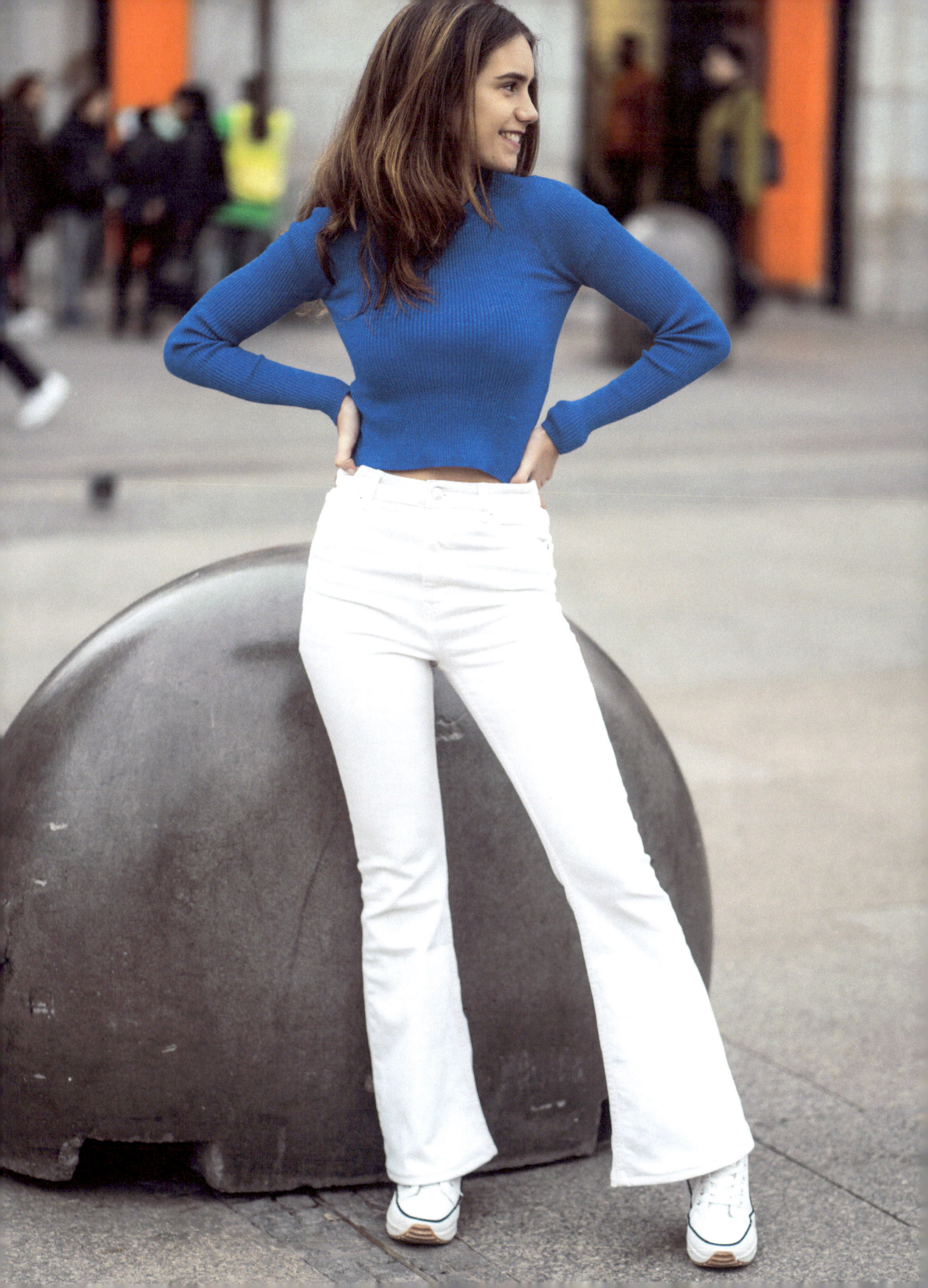

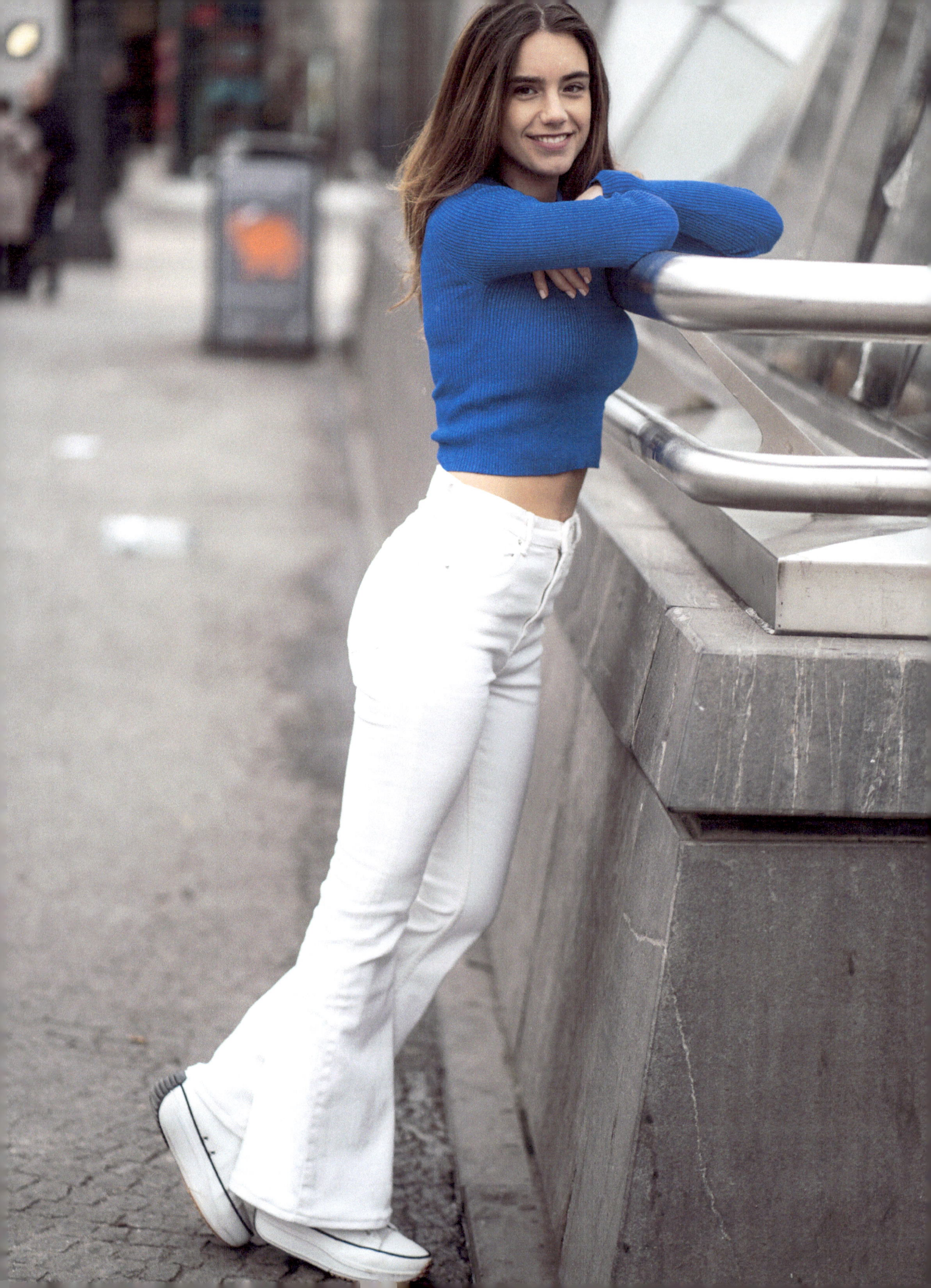

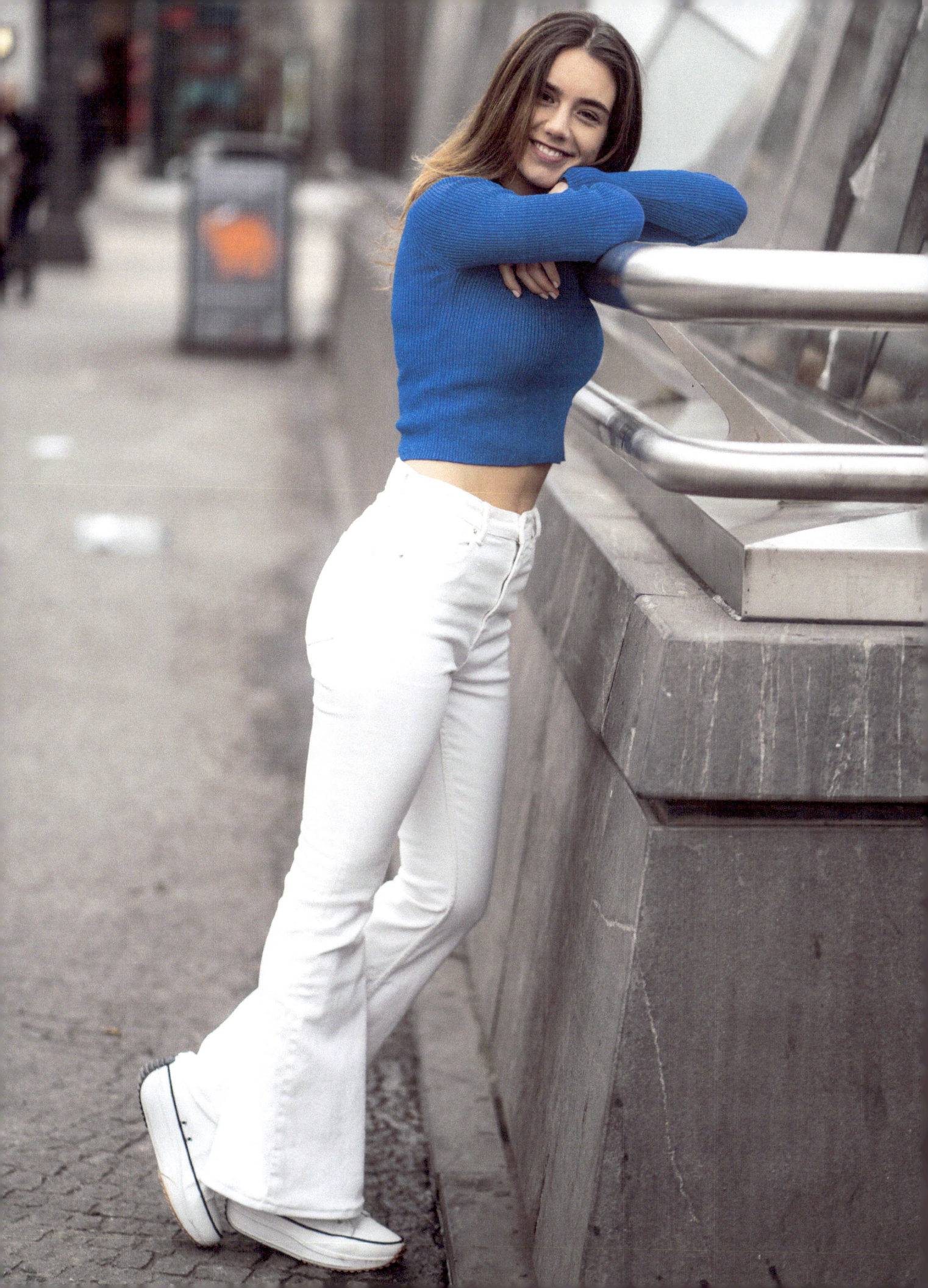

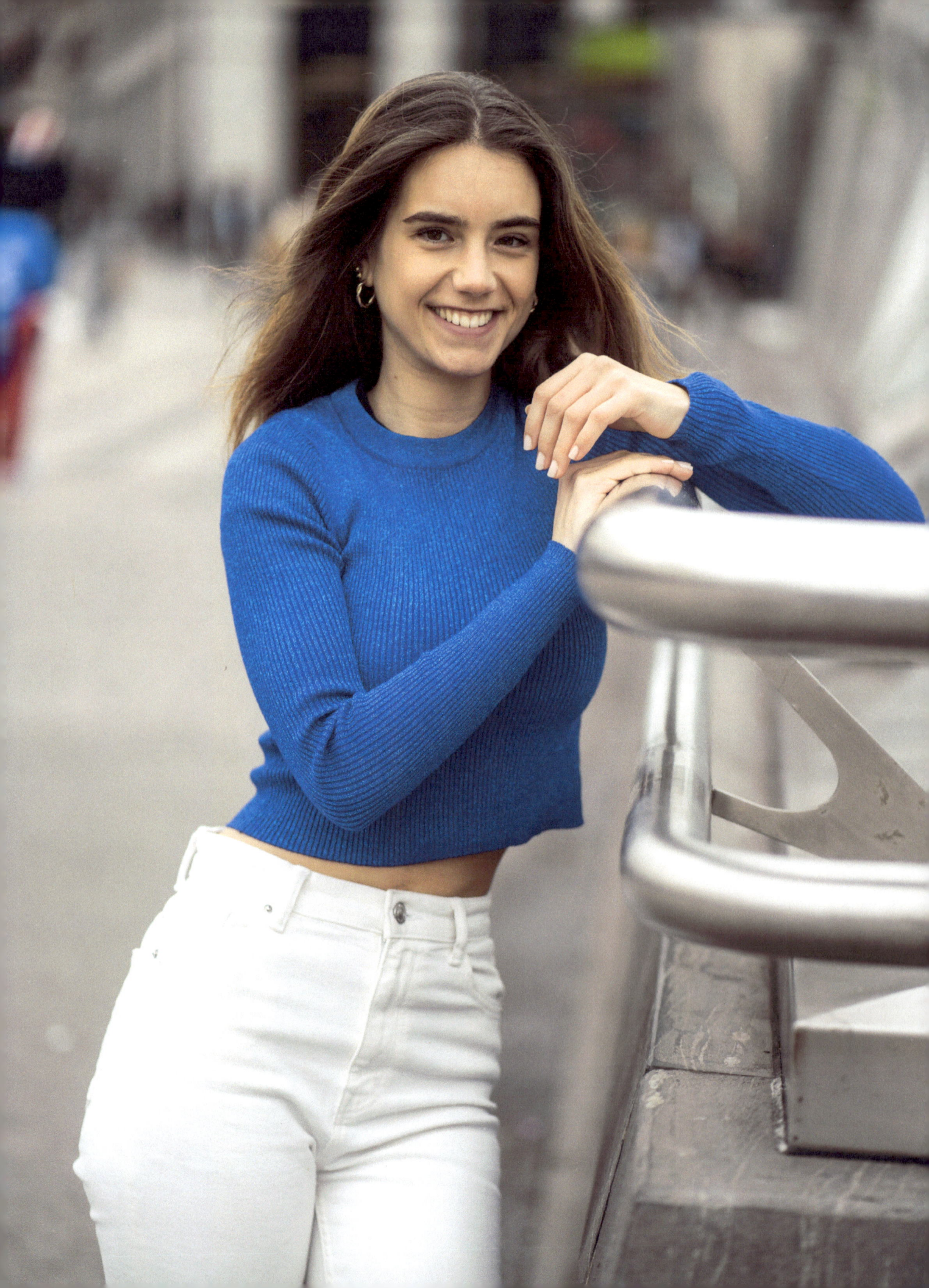

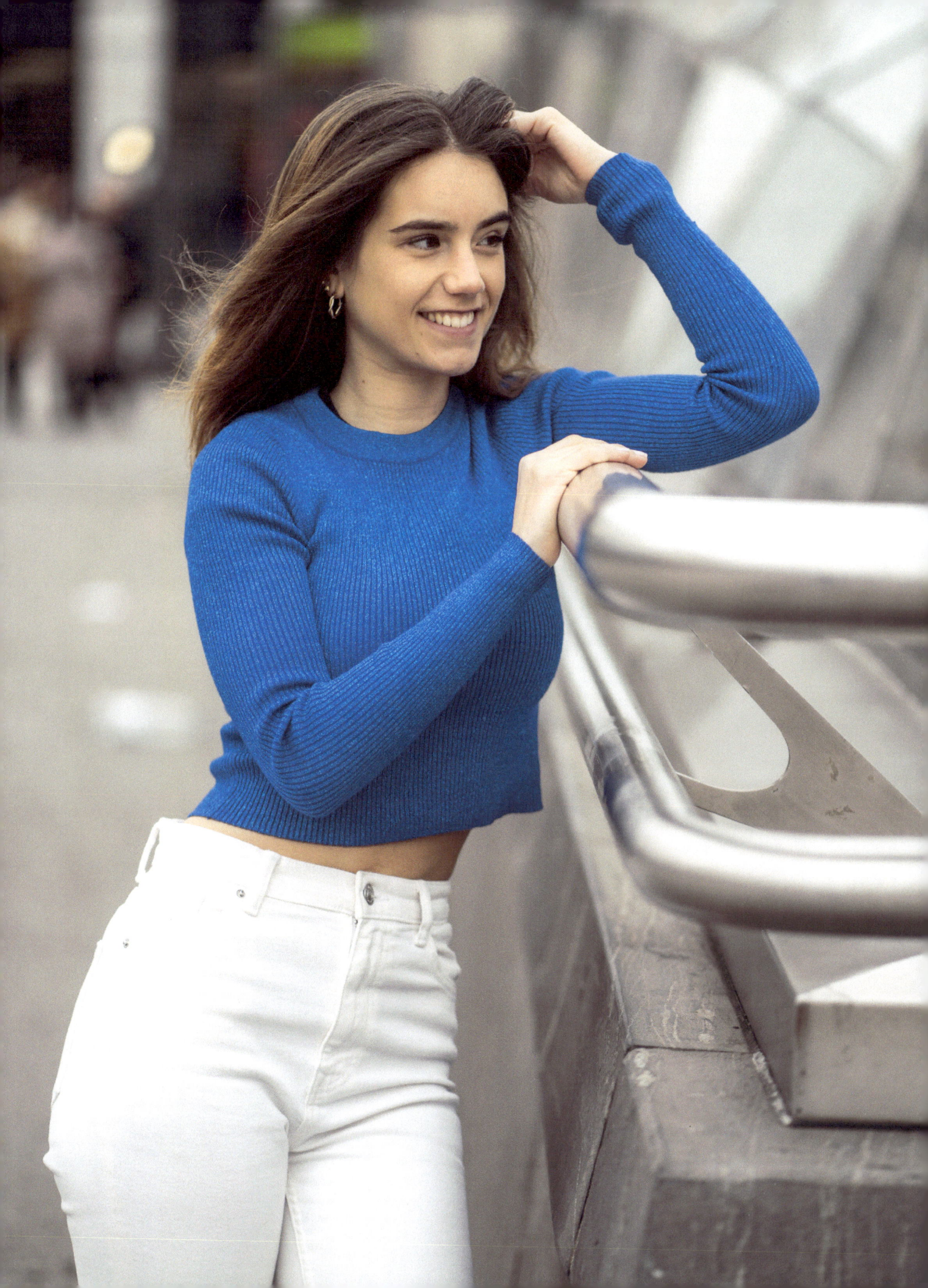

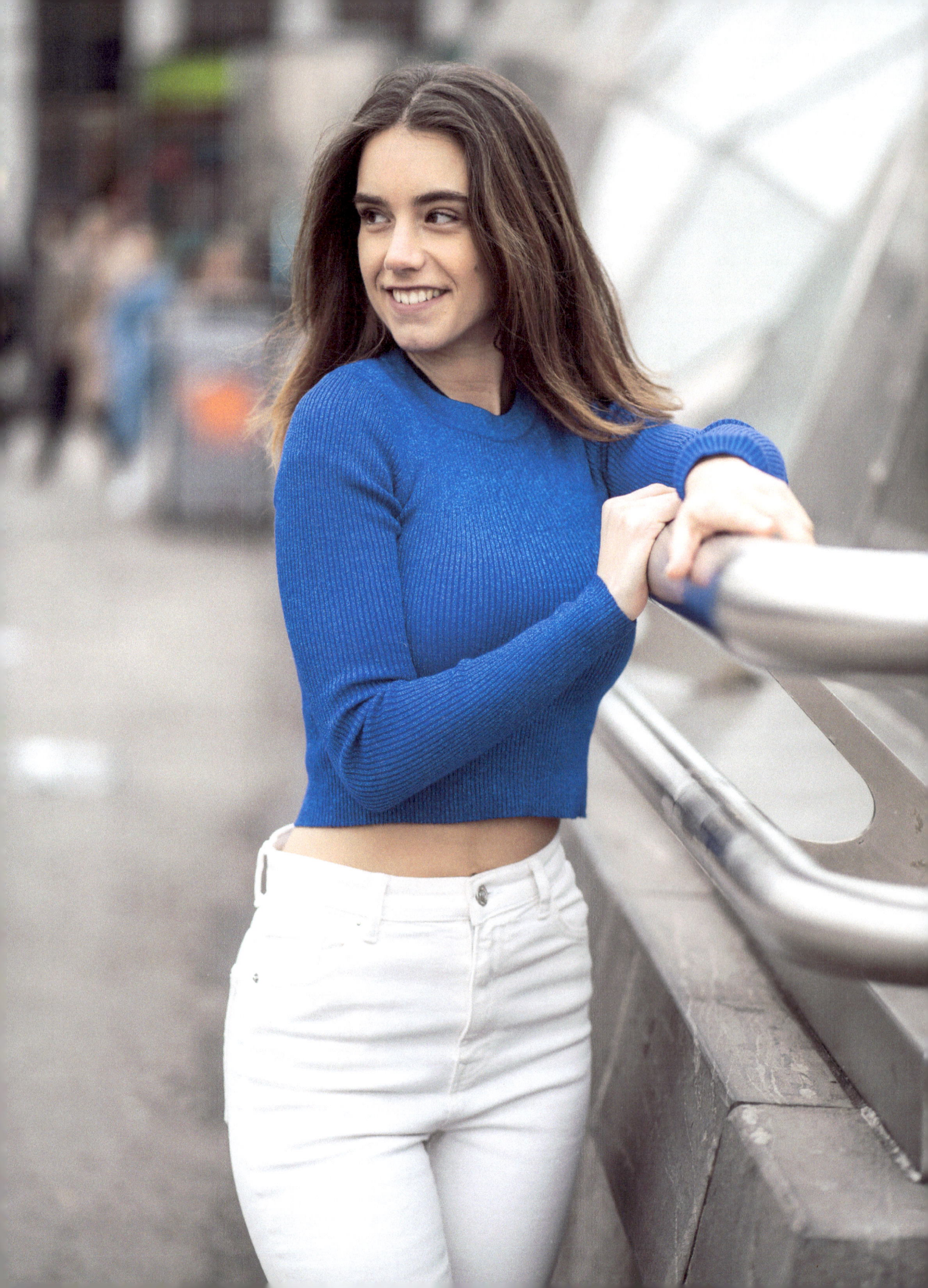

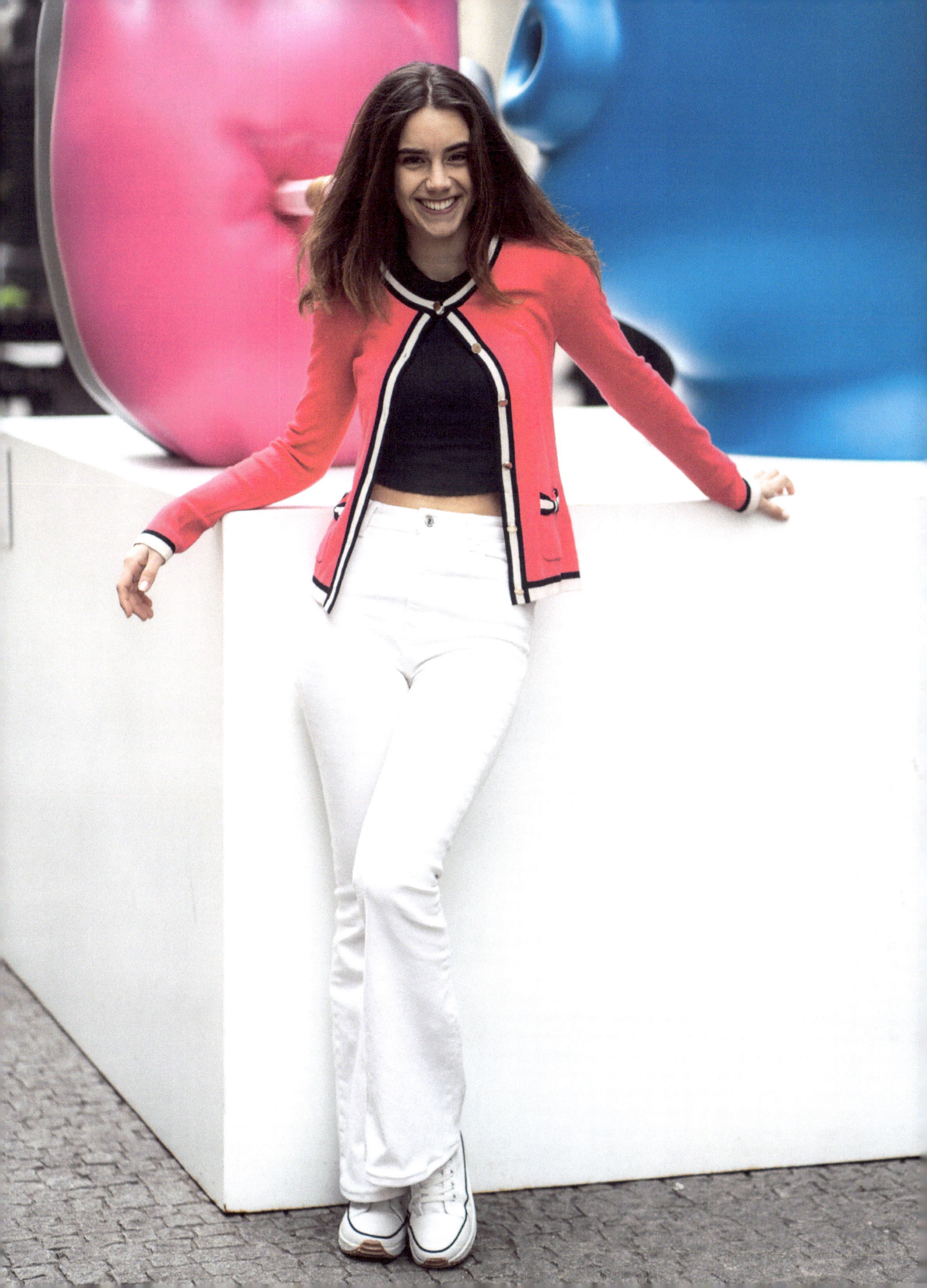

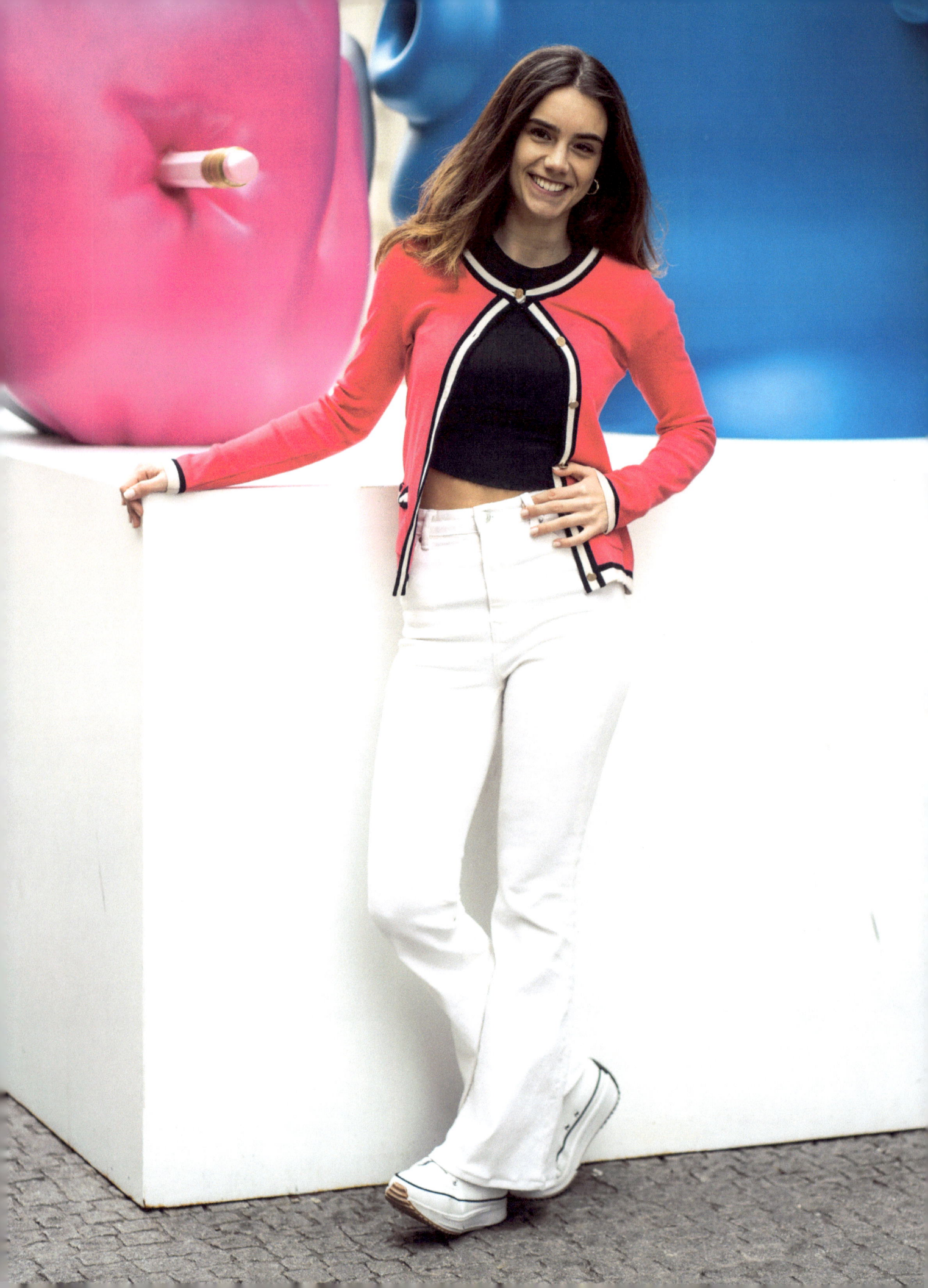

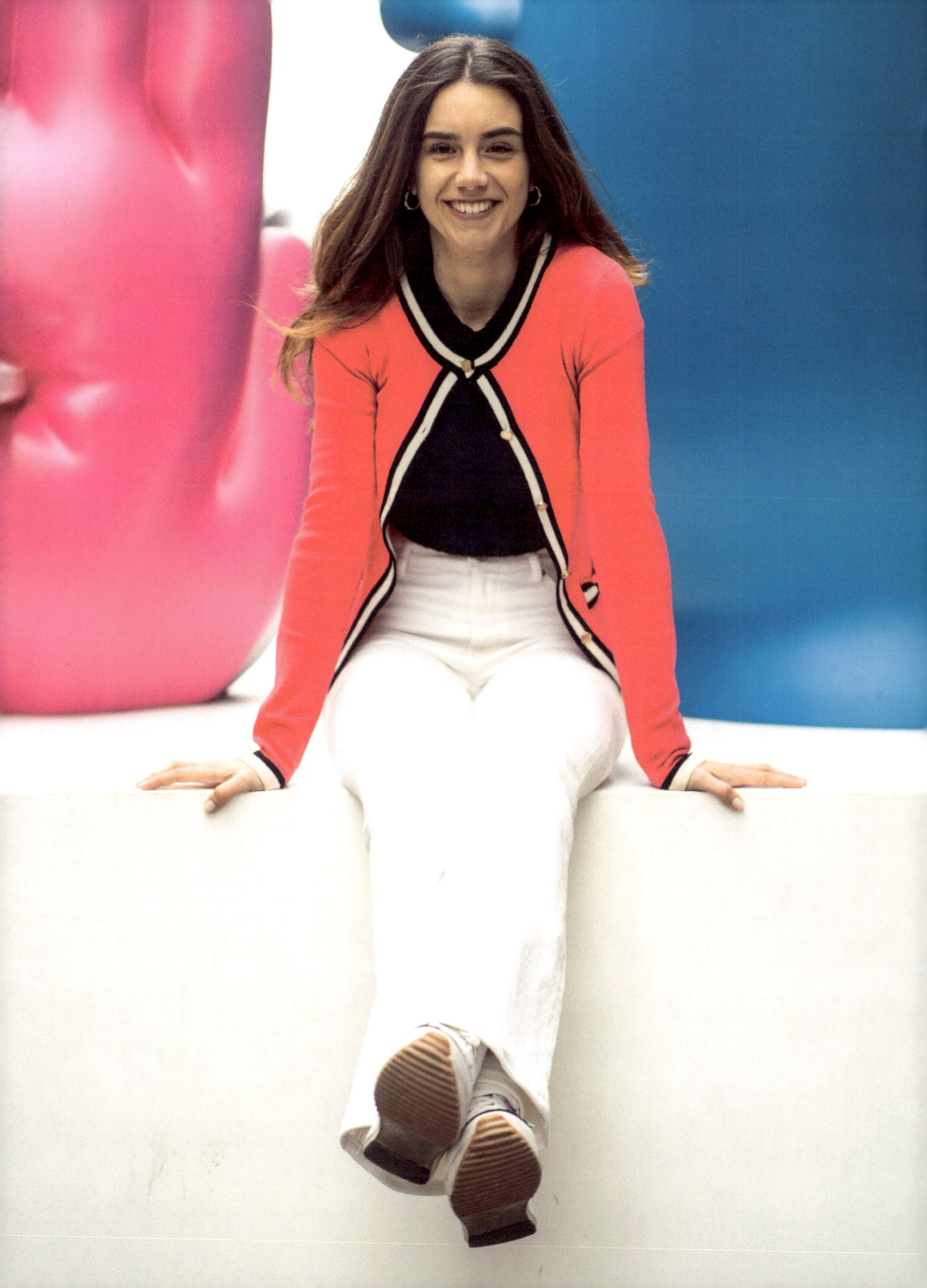

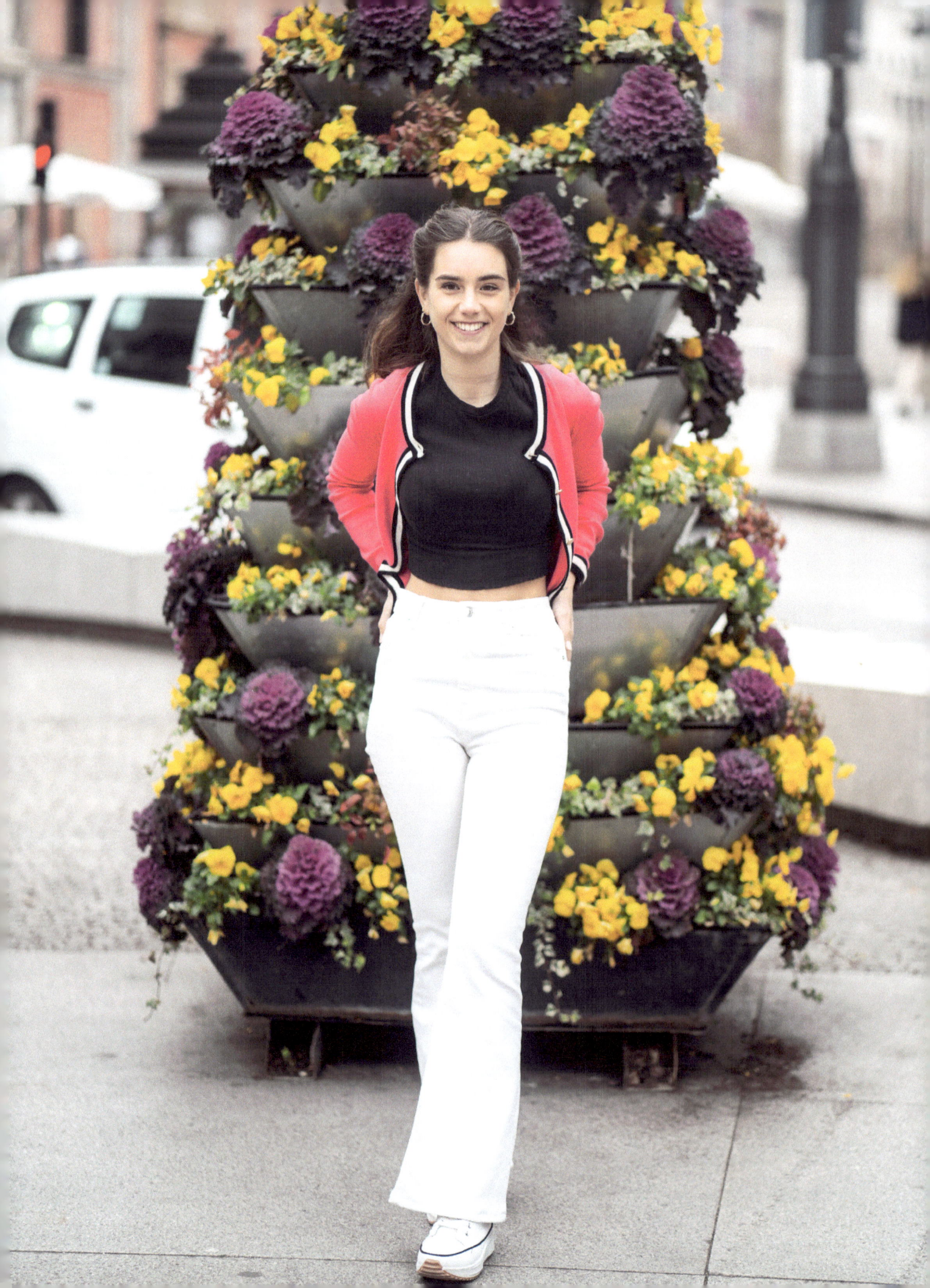

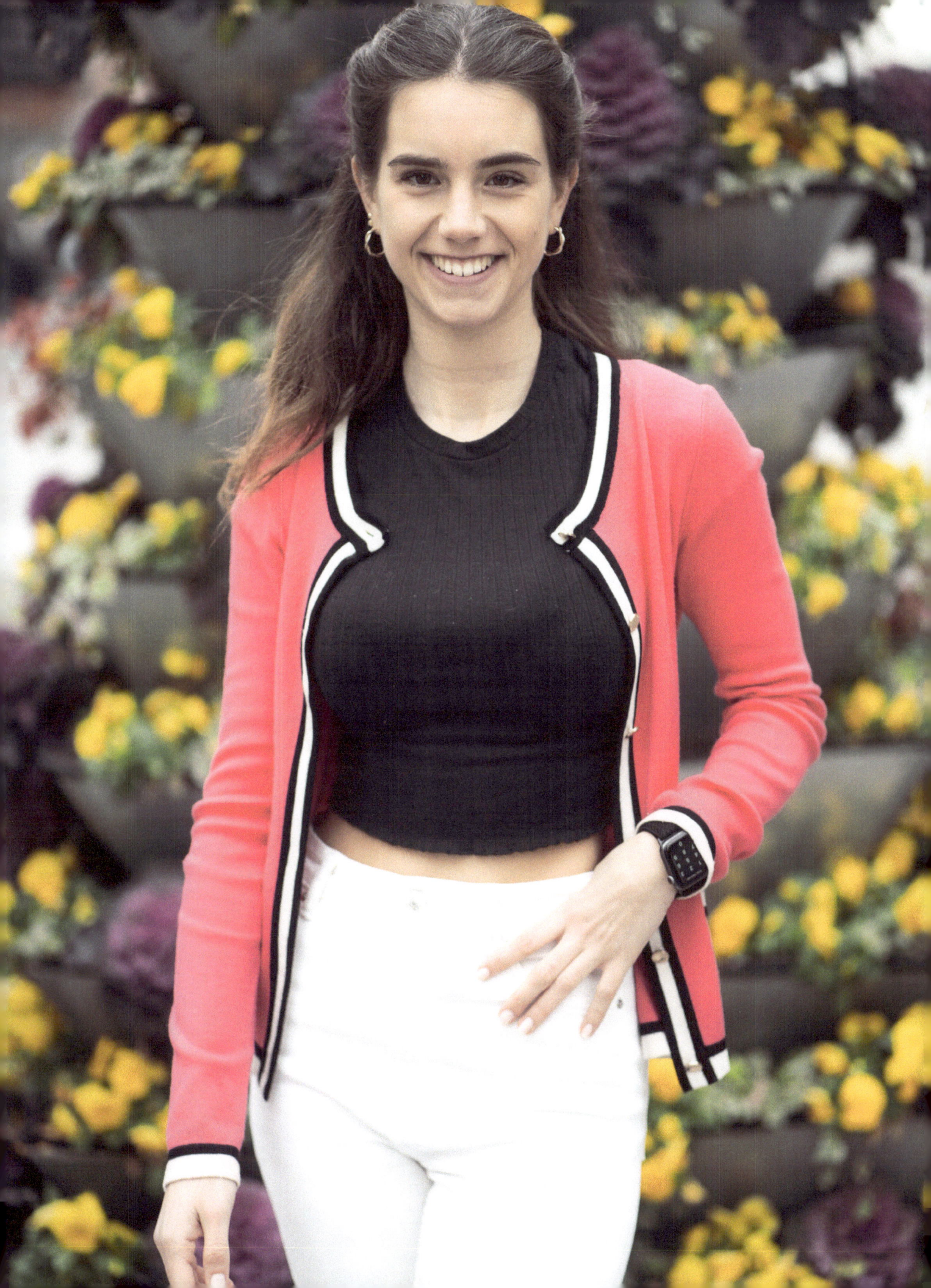

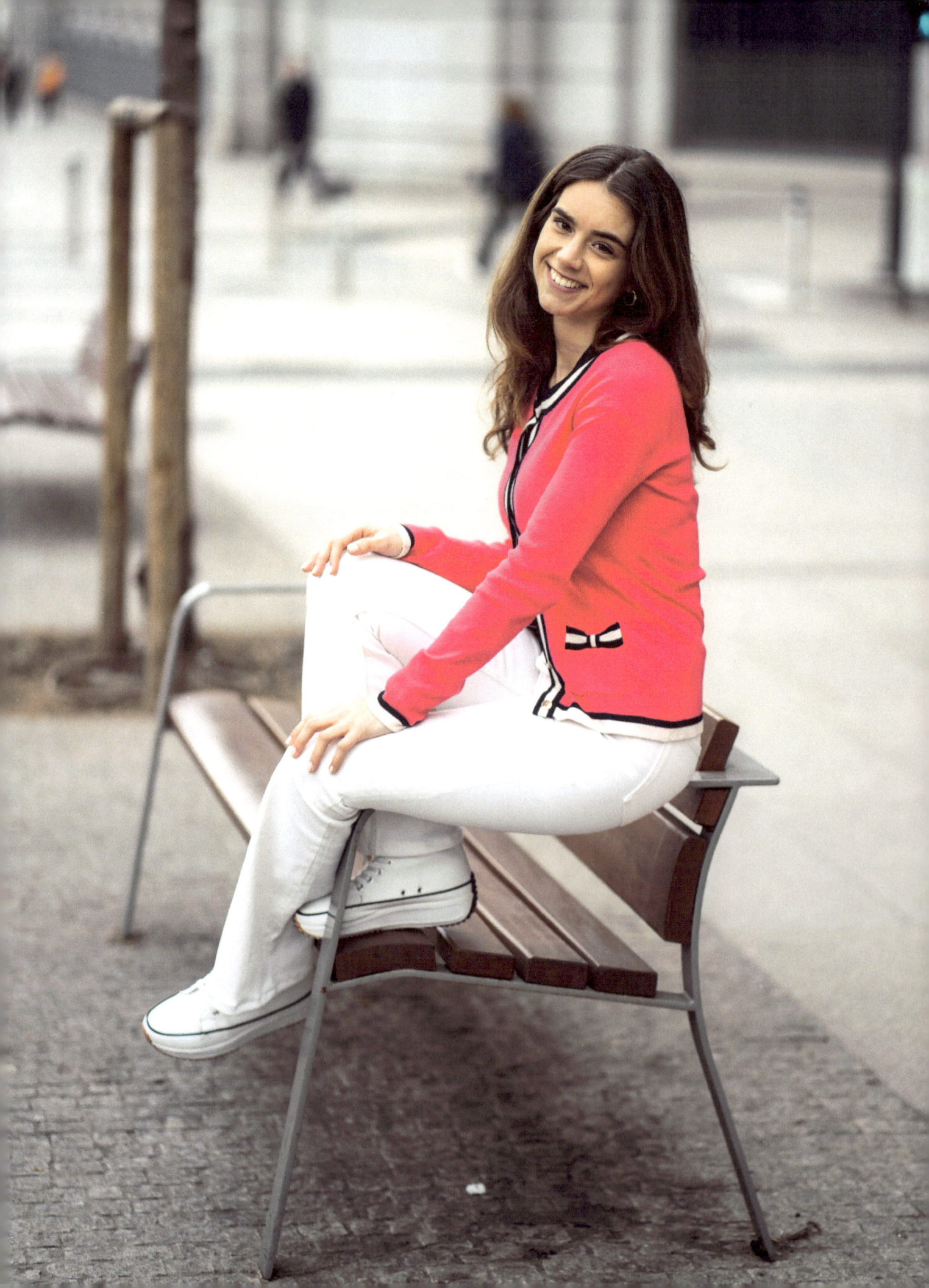

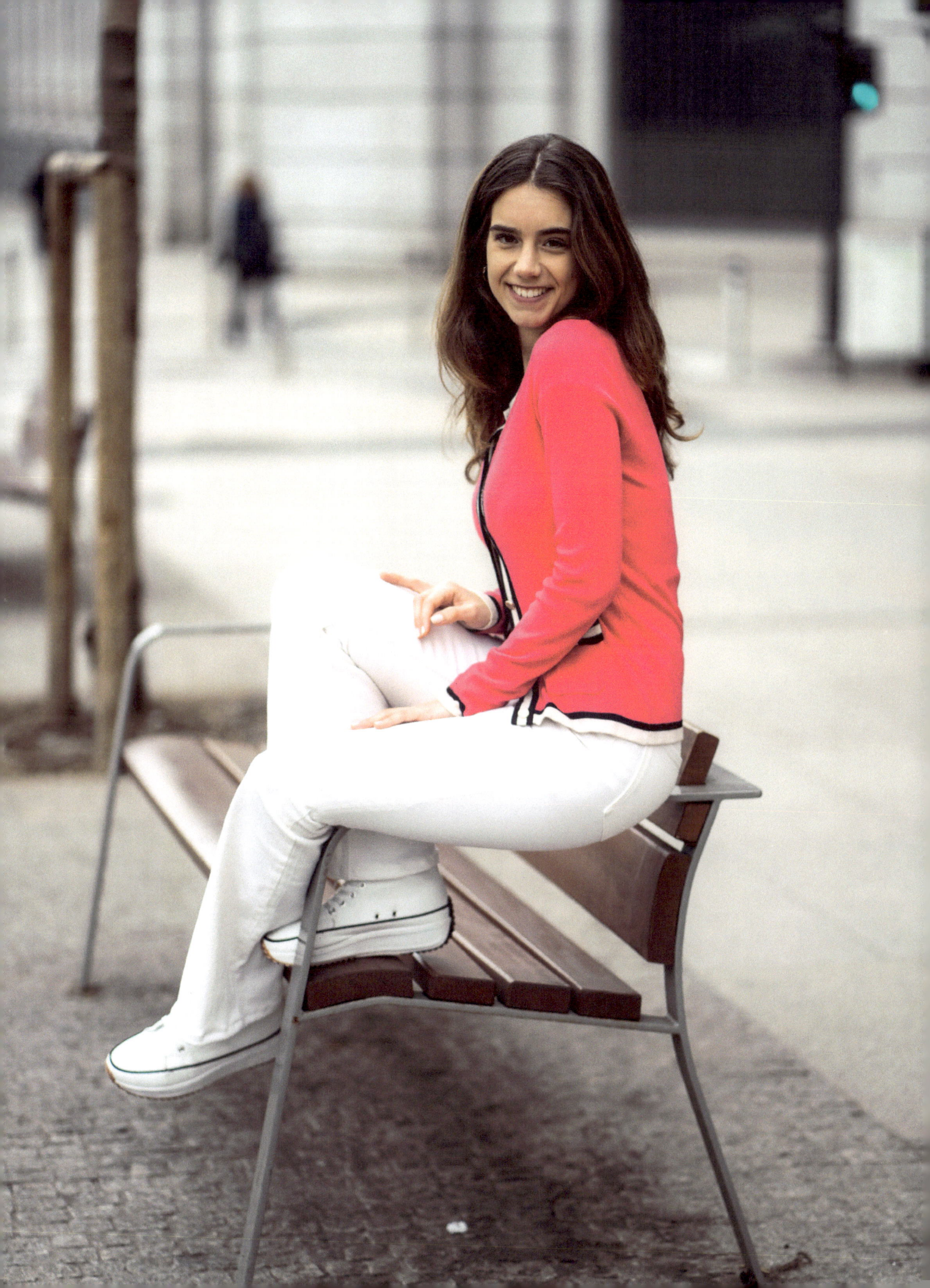

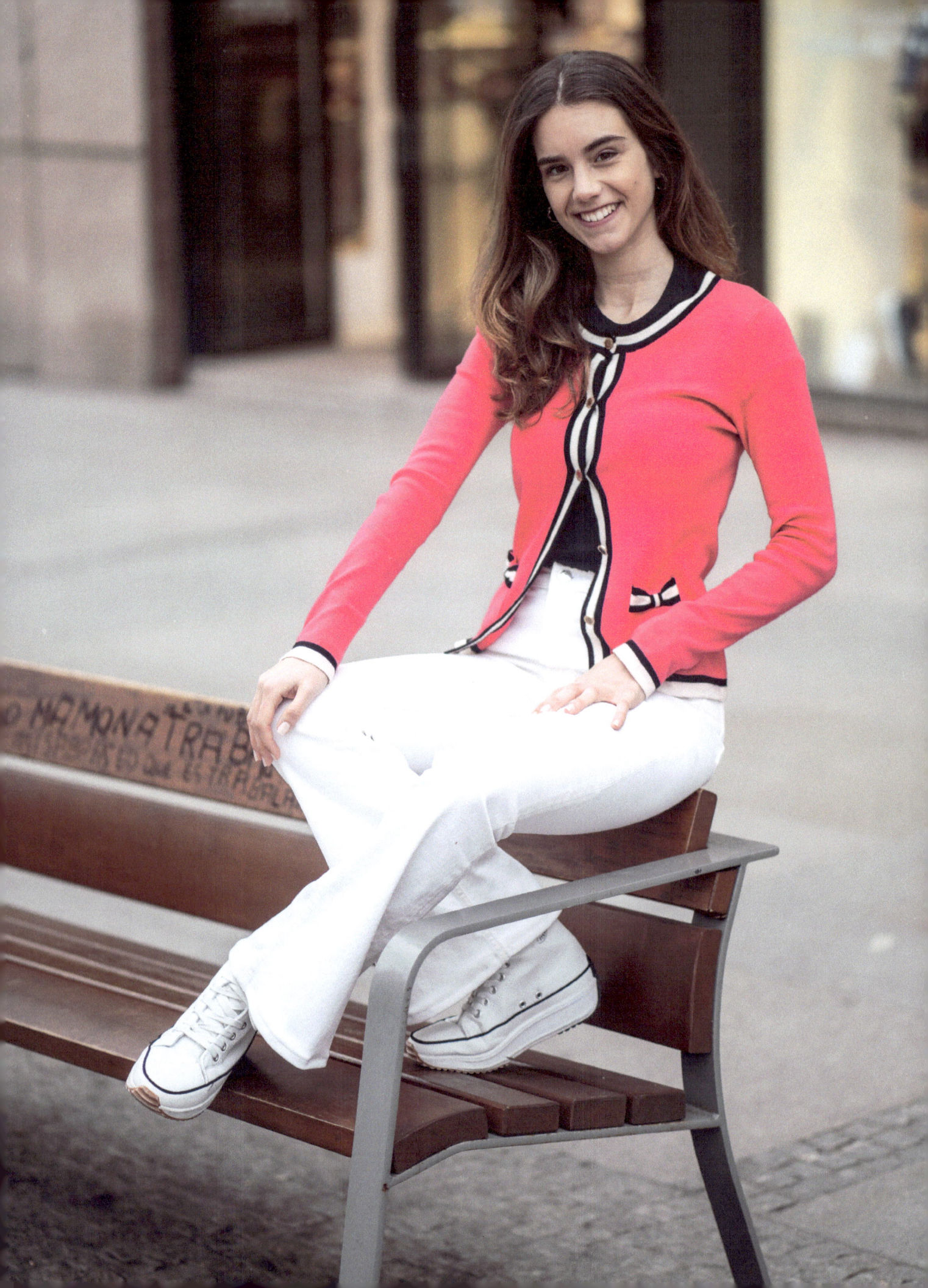

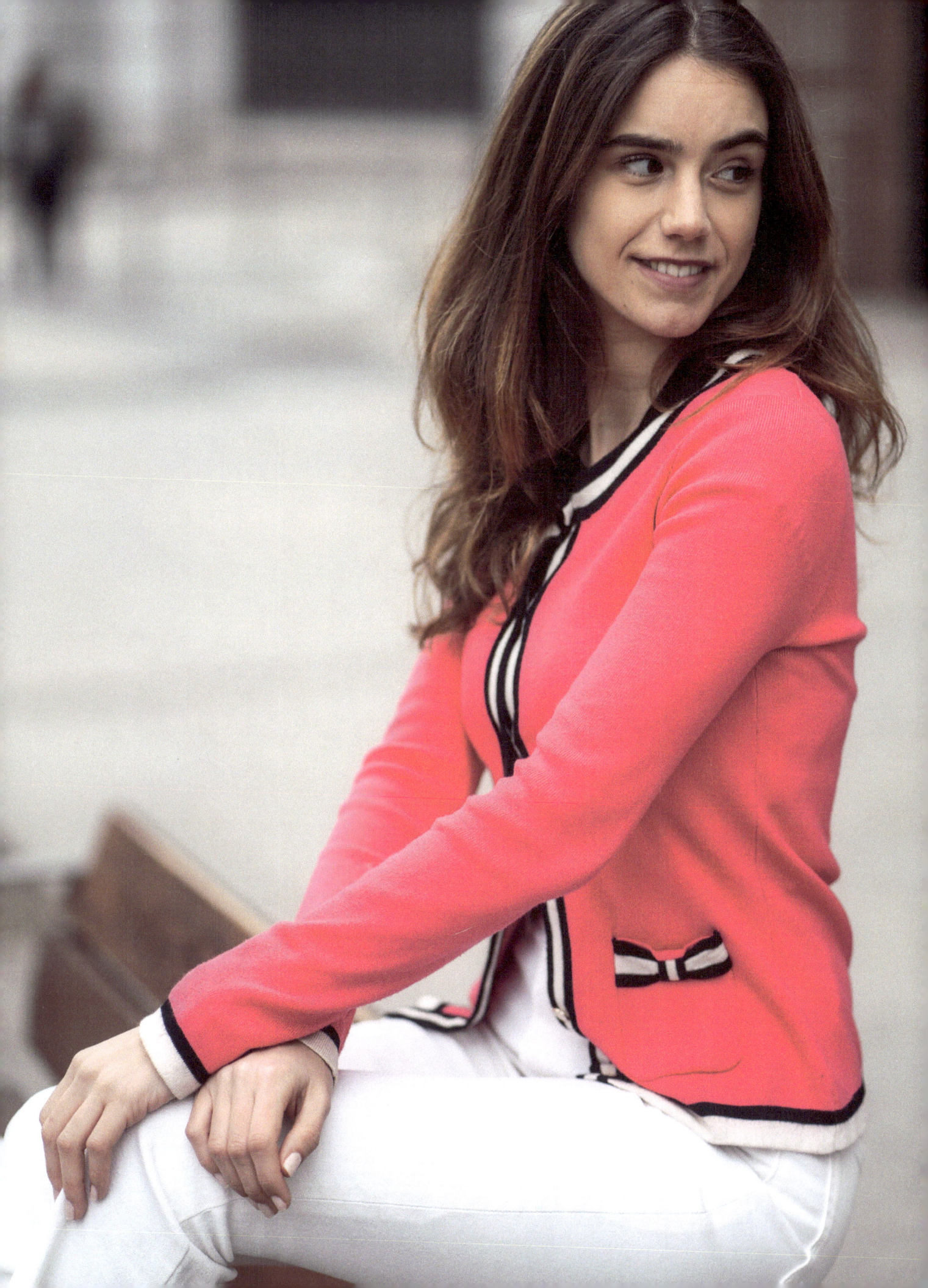

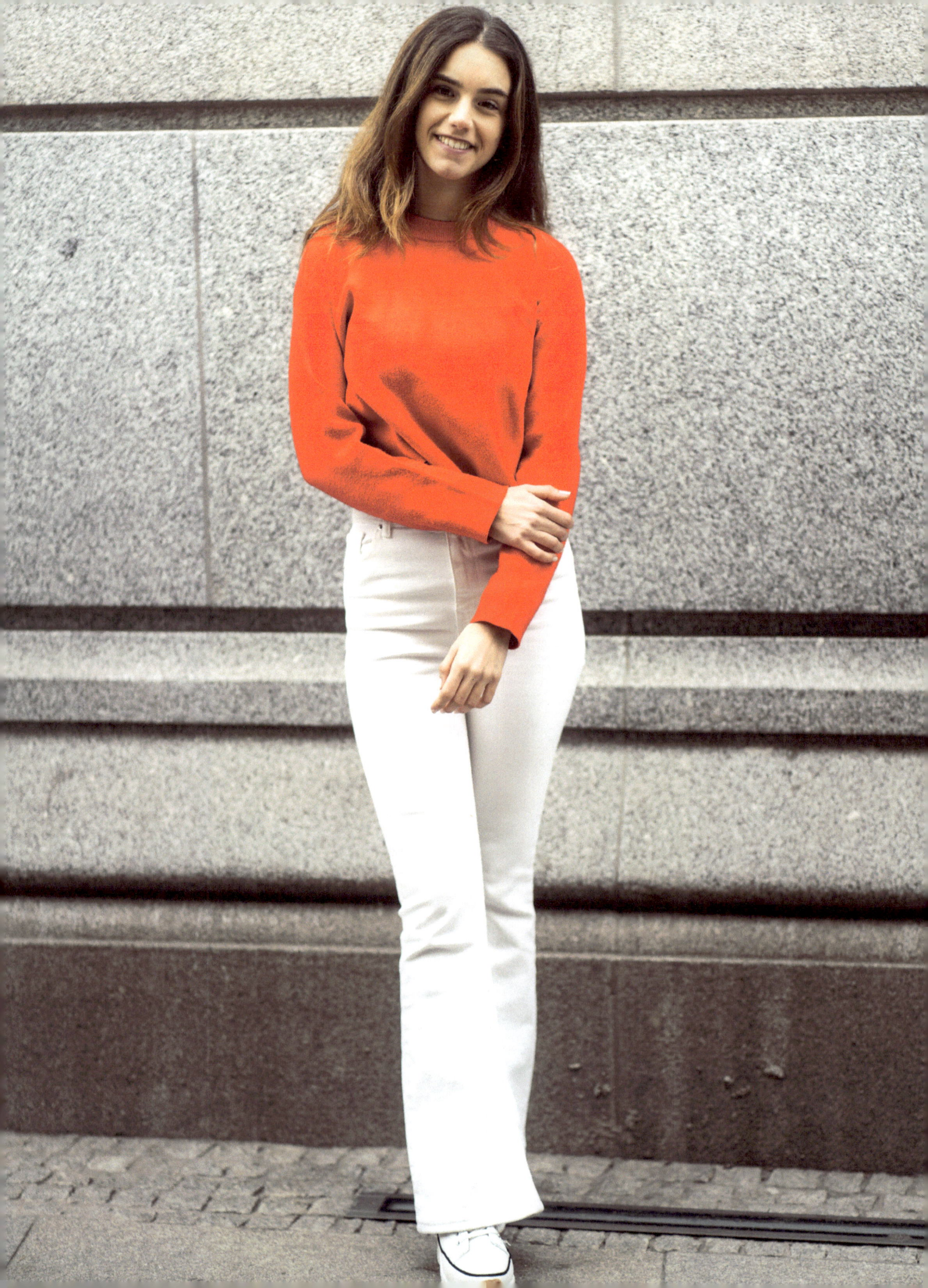

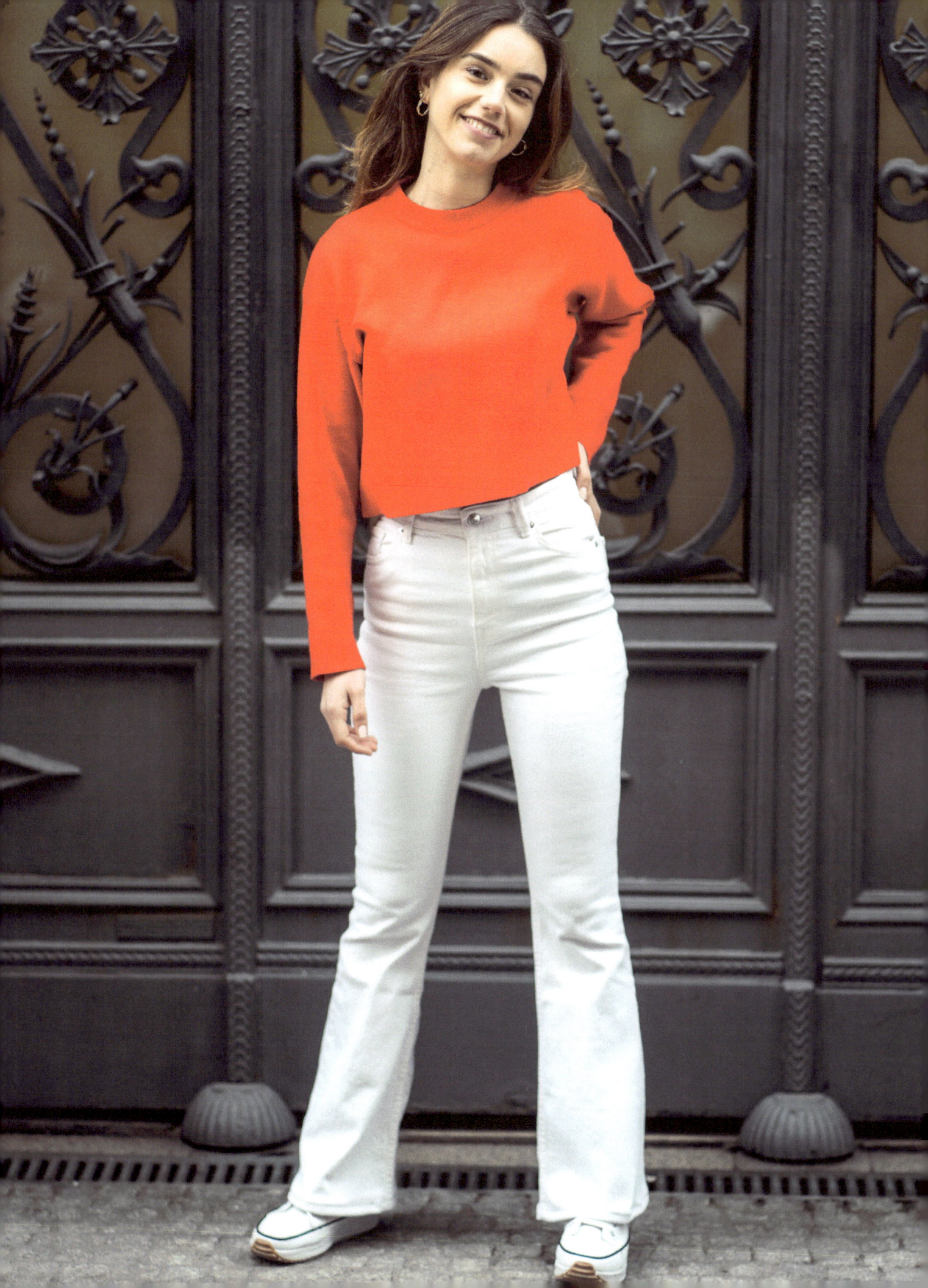

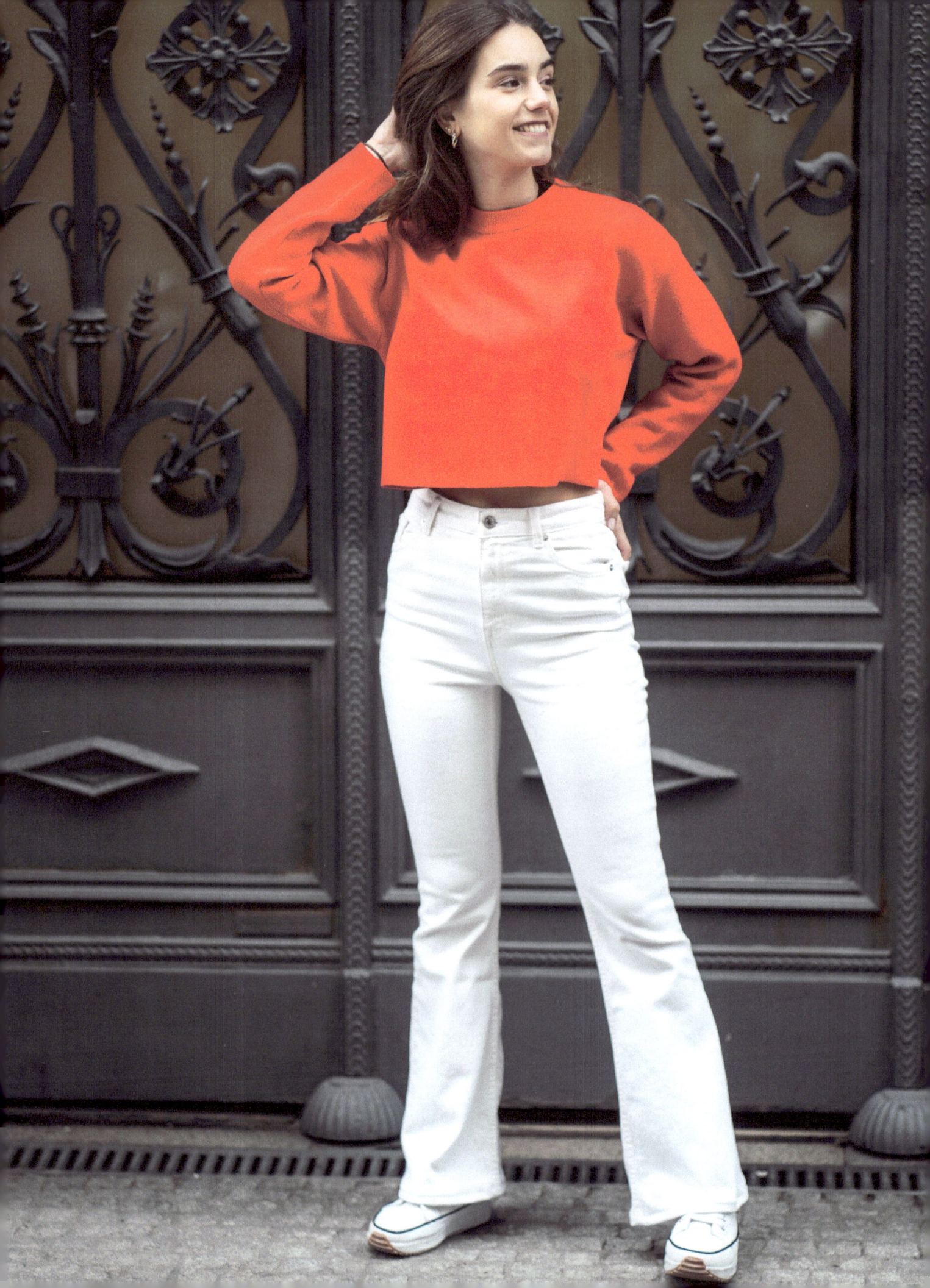

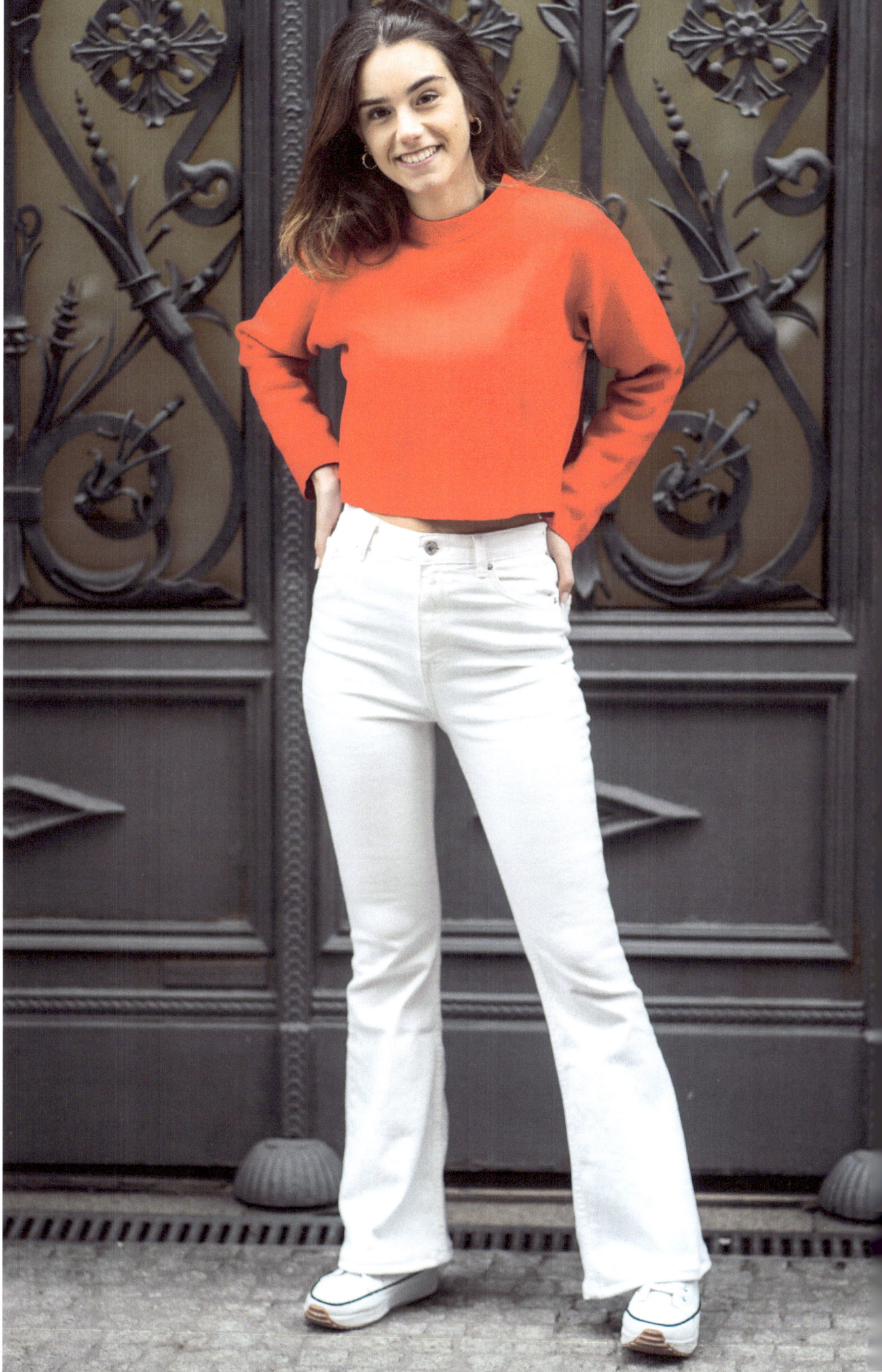

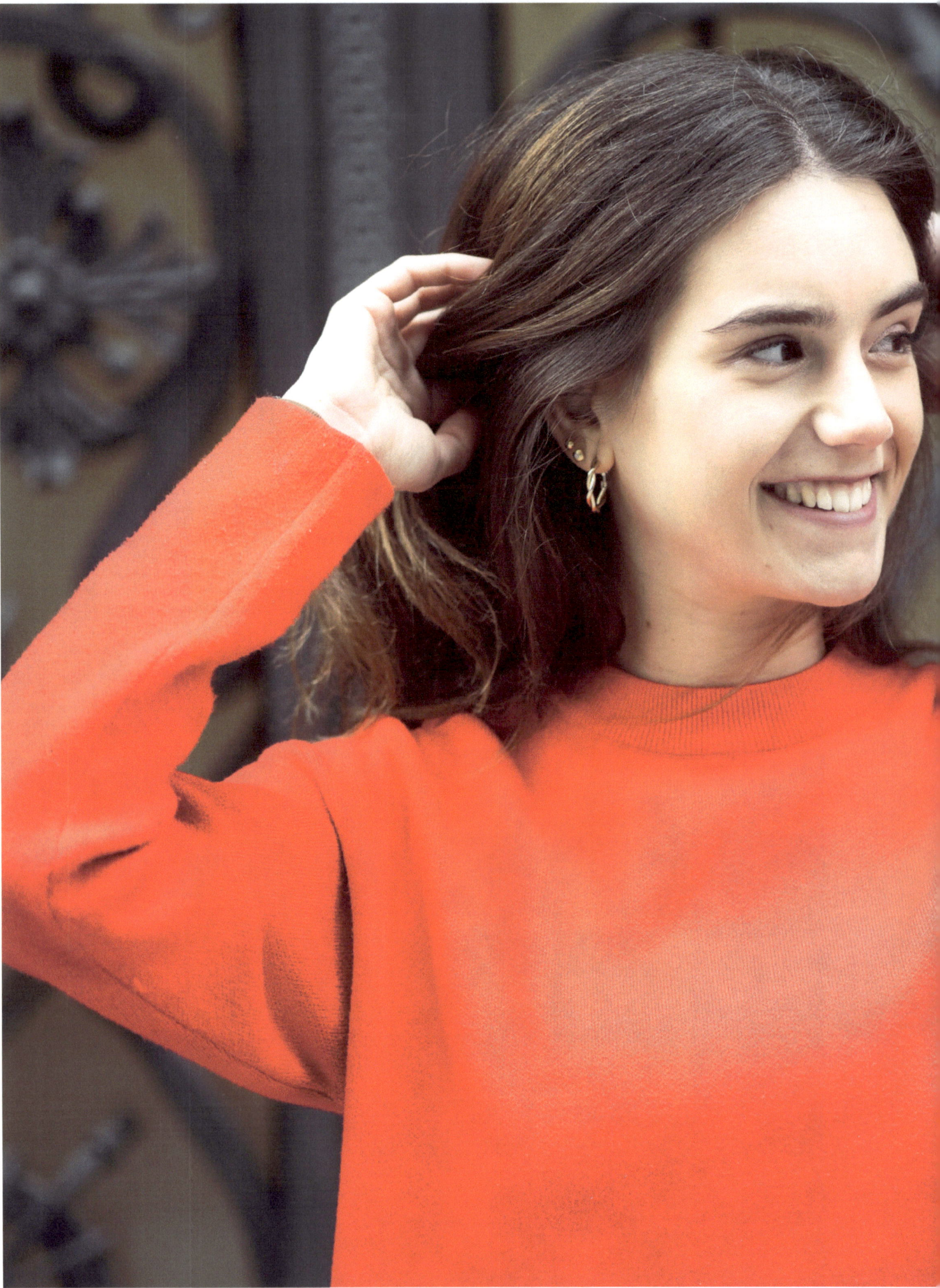

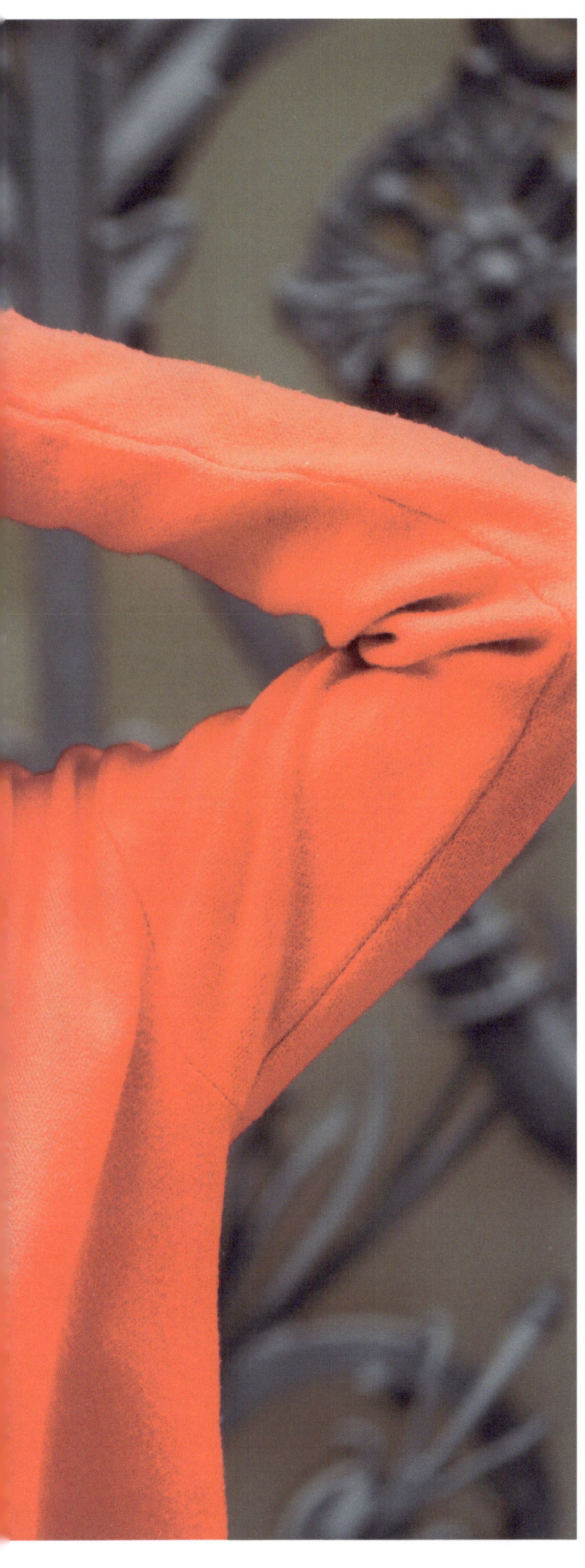

TOH

THE TRY ON HAUL MAGAZINE

By

Emporio Foto